FIVE ROADS TO FREEDOM

'Genius has been described as a supreme capacity for taking trouble. It might more fitly be described as a supreme capacity for getting its possessors into trouble.' On either count, it must be acknowledged that George Beeson was a genius among escapers in the Second World War. He took infinite trouble over all his attempts to regain his freedom and throughout his captivity he was almost permanently in trouble with his captors. Although his efforts to outwit the Germans were finally crowned with success, the situation in which he then found himself was almost as extraordinary as the adventures which had led him there.

George Beeson M.M.

Five Roads To
Freedom

CORGI BOOKS
A DIVISION OF TRANSWORLD PUBLISHERS LTD

FIVE ROADS TO FREEDOM

A CORGI BOOK 0 552 10714 X

Originally published in Great Britain by
Leo Cooper Ltd.

PRINTING HISTORY
Leo Cooper edition published 1977
Corgi edition published 1978

Corgi Books are published by
Transworld Publishers Ltd.,
Century House, 61–63 Uxbridge Road,
Ealing, London W5 5SA

Made and printed in Great Britain by
Cox & Wyman Ltd, London, Reading and Fakenham

*This book is dedicated to
Marie Paule Tassart
now Mrs David Richards,
and to her mother,
Madame Tassart*

CONTENTS

INTRODUCTION

I AM in the corridor of a train – one of a great mass of human beings, mostly French or German. We are packed so closely it is difficult to raise an arm, and the air is suffocating and foul. There is no room to sit down or to eat (but we can't eat anyway, for the food we brought with us is finished); there is room to breathe, it seems, for we go on living. We are travelling south from Paris, and my companion, a girl called Marie Paule, says Freedom is at the end of the journey. Three months ago I escaped from Stalag 383, and still I am wandering in search of this thing called Freedom.

That was my fourth escape, and they said to me: 'Next time, Herr Beeson, it will be Dachau.' A young Prussian with a very serious expression is heaving propaganda pamphlets out of the window; a French boy, one of his assistants, is talking to me but I daren't answer him because I can't speak French well. There is something I am afraid of, but I can't think what it is; there is a little seed of fear inside me all the time as the train stops, and moves on, and stops again. But all this is only a dream and that is why I can't understand the fear.

Now the girl, Marie Paule, who has been leaning against me, sleeping, wakes and says, 'George, it's your turn to sleep.' And when she speaks I know that, though this may be a dream, it is true; and I don't want it to be otherwise.

But the corridor is all black now and has become a cattle truck and there is a loathsome stench, and I look for Marie Paule and she isn't there. And there are men in the darkness crying for water, and I know that this is Poland and that at the end of the journey there is captivity.

It is a long time now since September, 1944, when I first saw England again, but I still dream. At first I didn't dream

9

at all, because to be awake was still not to be wholly awake. I wonder if you can understand that. I did not then understand it myself, and when I was talking to my friends I saw them begin to look bewildered, and they would ask me to repeat myself and try to keep calm. I realize now that I had not then any proper sense of time or proportion. Everything that had happened in five-and-a-half years was jumbled up in a great heap in my mind, and I took out great handfuls of it to show to my friends instead of a little bit at a time in its proper sequence. The release which had come to my body had not yet come to my mind.

Sometimes, my dreams are horrible; of a young Maquis lad with his hands chopped off at the wrist; of friends who died; of German swine I would sooner forget. Sometimes they are all of escape, and I see myself again disguised as a German Sergeant-Major locked in a louse-ridden cell at the top of Stuttgart police station as all-too-accurate bombs fall from our own planes; or endlessly tunnelling and endlessly being discovered; or climbing, desperately weary, over the Vosges mountains by night; or, dressed as a Frenchman, making a dash for a French camp. But my most enjoyable dreams are of my life with the Maquis, fighting in the open at last after years of hidden struggle and humiliation.

Of these, and many other things, I want to tell you – from the time of my capture in May, 1940, to the happy ending in the Mitchell bomber which finally lifted me out of Europe.

CHAPTER ONE

CAPTURE

ON the Thursday of the first week of the war which was the first week in September, 1939, I said to my brother, 'Come on Walter, let us go and join up and help get this lot over'; he said, 'Yes, come on; let's go.' First we had to go to Chiswick and tell Eileen, my fiancée, what we were going to do. I told Eileen, 'I am going to volunteer – so is Walter.' I tried for my brother to come with me in the same regiment as we both wanted to go in the Royal Army Ordnance Corps, but they would only take me as my brother was not old enough. The Recruiting Officer explained that at a later date I could put in an application for him to be transferred to my unit. Walter went to Colchester and I went to Hillsea.

When I reported into Hillsea, all the accommodation was filled up. We were issued with blankets and had to find somewhere to sleep, any place we could find some shelter. This was my first experience of the Army. I slept against a wooden building, near the barrack square. The next day I went before the Commanding Officer and he asked if I was an Engineer. I said I was. He then said I had to go to the training centre and pass a trade test. I went there and found the Chief Instructor and told him I had come for a first-class trade test for Fitter MV. He asked me what I had done. I said I had used a Van-Norman Boring Bar and a Huto Grinder and that I could use micrometers and various delicate instruments. So he gave me an inside and outside micrometer and said, 'Set that engine up – put that bar in and set it up as if you are going to grind or cut out the main bearings.' Anyway, he passed me and I became Fitter MV First Class. They gave me three stripes, and so I was a Sergeant in the Royal Army Ordnance Corps. I really wanted to get to the Royal Army Service Corps, so I made an application for an interview with the Commanding Officer and I said I wanted to join the Royal Army Service Corps because my brother was there. The Commanding Officer agreed to make arrangements for me to go and see Colonel Leyland, the Commanding Officer at Portsmouth. I went and saw him, and he agreed to send me to Colchester, to go on the Officer's Training Course because at Aylesbury Grammar School I had been in the OTC. So I came back to Hillsea Barracks and stayed the night. The next day I went and looked at Orders, and there I saw my name. I was on draft to the 8th Army Field Workshops which was attached to the Tank Corps at Warminster. I saw the Adjutant and said, 'I am due to go to Colchester.' He said, 'Oh that doesn't matter; you go to Warminster where you are detailed and you will be posted to the Royal Army Service Corps as soon as possible.'

I arrived at Warminster; the next day I was kitted out and the next day we were on the move to France, with our convoy of recovery vehicles, Scammels and Leylands.

The Scammels and Leylands were the Rolls-Royce of heavy vehicles. Some of the vehicles were for recovery of tanks and any type of vehicles that needed help of any description, whether it was upside down, or in a river, we had the equipment to recover it and it was a very interesting and worthwhile job. The Leylands were mobile factories. Some vehicles had lathes and machines for making parts. There was one vehicle which housed a generating plant for making electricity.

After our vehicles had been loaded at Southampton on to a cargo boat, the personnel embarked on a troop carrier. This was a most terrifying experience. The first thing that happened was that we were taken below the water line of the ship and placed in a very small compartment where there were three sets of three-tier bunks, with very little room. The most frightening thing for me was when the Petty Officer came into our small quarters and showed us how and where to push the control for closing the watertight doors. It was explained to us that should we be hit by a submarine this door would be our means of survival.

We sailed from Southampton at dusk. Between ten and eleven at night I had to take my party on deck. We were issued with life jackets and a rope was fixed round part of the structure of the ship for men to hang on to. There were many men on deck who were very sea sick, and it was a difficult job to help anyone.

The reason for our being on deck was that the ship was trying to evade a German U-boat. I was not ill but I stank like a polecat from the vomiting of men that I was helping. The sea was quite rough and the night seemed to have a dirty, sinister darkness; out there somewhere the enemy was waiting to sink us. The thing that I remember most of all was my relief at coming away from the compartment below.

While on deck I was not afraid. My life jacket strapped around me gave me a great sense of security.

We had been nearly two days on the boat and when we arrived at Cherbourg we were all very hungry and had to queue to get some soup.

After all our equipment had been unloaded, we journeyed to Rennes and there we stopped and found billets in farm-yards at Oiseau-le-Petit. From there we moved up to the Somme and it was here that I got jaundice and was sent to Le Tréport Hospital. I was there for about twenty-three days and so I lost my regiment and had to go right down to La Baule. This camp was a transit camp, where men who had lost their units for some reason or another were allo-cated to other units. So I found myself in the 14th Army Field Workshops around Carvin, the centre of the French coalfields.

From here we moved up to attack the Germans, but we were forced back until we got to St. Malo where we were captured. This came about so very quickly; we were about to go over a level crossing, when suddenly two German tanks, which were hidden behind a very thick hedge, opened up on us and killed our Commanding Officer and all those in his car. Then our ammunition wagon went up and we all had to shift out from our vehicles and take cover in the hedge and try to do battle. When it became dark we managed to get into some houses further up the road. But it was useless. We were a non-combatant unit; we had nothing apart from our old rifles and so we decided that we would try and break through in groups and find out where we were and what was going on, because actually with the British Expeditionary Force nobody knew anything.

I was lying in a ditch and I was very wet. The ground rose in front of me for about fifty yards and it must then have fallen away very steeply. At the ridge of this mound I saw something move, so I took aim and fired. A horse kicked up his hind legs and galloped away; my shot must have clipped his mane. I scrambled through a hedge, the Germans were throwing out their lights and it made the place like daylight. I crawled along the hedge and came to a village. I managed to get into the church and I thought that if I climbed up to the belfry I would get some idea of what was happening and where I could possibly go. So I climbed to the belfry, fell asleep and was awakened by the frightening crash of the bell ringing for people to go to Mass. It was Sunday, so I waited there all day. Nothing happened although I could see buildings on fire, I could hear machine-guns and see the German planes coming over and bombing. I waited there until the next day, and in the morning a verger came in. I told him I was a British soldier and asked if he knew of a person who could hide me until I could manage to get away. He said 'No'. He knew of no one but he would get the two Sisters from the Convent who came to do work here prior to Mass. He fetched the Sisters and they collected me from the belfry and one of the Sisters was really charming – absolutely lovely – and she asked if I was cold or hungry. To my reply of 'Yes', she told me to wait there and she went away and returned with two bottles of soup and a piece of bread. When she gave me those bottles, my hands were so cold, that I could not hold them and accidentally dropped one. The other Sister was very cross. However, I took the soup and went back up to the belfry.

14

The next day the man came and said that he could find no way to help me and that I would have to go away from the belfry because the Germans would come and find me and then it would put the church in a difficult position and probably the Nuns also. So when it was dusk, I climbed out from my hiding place, down through the church, on to the road. The road was clear with no one in sight, when unexpectedly up came a German motor-bike, with a machine-gun on the side-car; they pulled up in front of me and they asked where I was going. I did not understand what they had said as they spoke a kind of pidgin English – and so they made me sit on the back of the motor-bike and took me to a collecting camp where there were other men of my unit and soldiers of other regiments. That was where we stayed for a couple of days.

Then the Germans rounded us all up and started us on a march. We walked and we walked, with no food. The 51st Division were still engaged with the Germans and so they were forced to march us anywhere they could. We had to walk miles and miles and miles – all round Amiens, all round Arras, right the way through to Belgium. Now in this time we had been given no food whatsoever. The only food that we had had was what the French women had thrown to us as we marched along the road and some green-stuff that we had picked from the hedges. It was not until we got to the borders of Belgium that the Germans stopped us and marched us into a field. By this time there were somewhere in the region of 15,000 men – French, Belgian, British – and that was where they rested us for that night. They set up a kind of a cookhouse; this was two big old baths. Each bath contained a horse's head, plus a few old potatoes and some funny bits of green vegetables, and the sight of this made most of us vomit. It was a terrible sight and as we passed by the bath of soup, a bit further on there were trestles made up, and on these was green bread and we had a fifth of a loaf of green bread each and that was the first meal given to us by the Germans.

Now I must go back along the route we followed, that is the route from France to Belgium. The roads everywhere were dilapidated, bombed and shelled to pieces; there were

15

dead horses, dead personnel. The horses had been lying there for days, they were swollen and stunk to high heaven and some of the horses of the French Army Service Corps had parts cut away which were being used to make stews with. It is impossible for anybody to appreciate the waste of both animal and human life and the complete annihilation of villages all along the route. In one particular case I saw a beautiful farm with a wonderful herd of Fresian cattle, and there in the middle of the yard the Germans had just roped a bull and slaughtered it and were about to skin it. It was a terrible sight to see – good-class stuff being wrongfully killed when other food could easily be supplied to the forces.

There was one instance which hurt very much – a man who had been walking just in front of me, a guardsman from the Welsh Guards, broke column to go on the verge of the road to relieve himself. The food that we had had was odd pieces of green bread, odd pieces of rhubarb, hawthorn from the hedgerows, or anything we could snap up, and of course our tummies were not in the best of conditions, and so this guardsman fell out on the side of the road to relieve himself and he was immediately shot by the Germans. That was the kind of treatment we received.

I can remember rushing into a house on the side of the road, finding a cupboard where there were two loaves of bread, so stale that they were green, and also there was some cheese with green fur on it and a lump of butter which was not so bad – but I nearly got shot as a German had seen me. I had just come from the house to join the column when he fired at me. Whether I was running too fast or whether he was a bad shot I don't know, but I soon hid myself among the other soldiers. The column was over five miles long and every so often the line of marchers was broken by an armoured car ready for action. On both sides of the road marched German soldiers who were relieved every hour and picked up by a lorry where they rested before coming back on to duty. Once going through a village I kicked a dustbin over and found a loaf of bread, green and dusty, but my mates and I ate it. Sometimes we had no breaks and many men fell asleep walking and fell to the ground to be aroused very smartly by the German guards. My mate and I took it in turns to sleep while we marched. Both being about the same height, one would put his head on the other's shoulder and each would hang on to one another.

The greatest problem to my way of thinking was when the column was rested for the night. Men's boots used to be stolen off their feet whilst they slept. To wake and find you had nothing on your feet to start the day with was something worse than being crucified. I remember that one foreign soldier was caught stealing boots and a German shot him. One must not lose sight of the fact that all we had was what we had been captured in, no greatcoat, no spare boots or clothing. So when it rained you just had to let your clothing dry out on you, and believe me we were wet through for days. Now the best way we found to keep warm – or try to – at night, was to sleep in threes, and to keep changing our positions as often as we needed. I always took my boots and socks off and tied them around my neck with the laces and used them as pillows. That stopped my boots from being stolen. When the Germans rested us for a night they made us all go into large fields and surrounded the fields with armoured cars and machine-guns and they then had a series of searchlights which kept playing on us all night long.

Going through a village one day there was a lot of noise caused by chickens, when suddenly between two houses about six chickens flew across the road into our column. Luckily for me I caught one. The others were caught by French Colonial troops. I pulled the head off mine and dragged it near the ground so that the blood could run out, and then I plucked it. When it had been dead for a day I started eating it and sharing it with my mate, without it being cooked. Believe me when you are really hungry you will eat anything.

The weather was a bit cold. Most of us had been captured without our mess tins, so we had nothing to collect water or food in. I found a rusty old jam tin in a ditch on the edge of a village; little did I know at the time what service this tin was to give to me. Nearly all the drinking water came from the French women in the villages as we passed through. They put buckets on the paths. Some people had put a bottle of wine in to give the water a bit of taste, I suppose, and these wonderful women also used to throw bread into our ranks. These women were very courageous because the Germans sometimes used to try and stop the French giving us things and they were butted, slapped and kicked and told, 'Not for the English, only for the French soldiers.' But many boys' lives were saved by these good French people.

The forced march was a terrible ordeal, both physically and mentally, because we were not the only ones on the march: there were the advancing Germans with their tanks and these often tried to run over us, or push us against a wall; there were the people evacuating from burned-out villages; there were the lines of communications of the Germans, and the roads were strewn with dead horses and mules. The French still had a lot of cavalry and used horse-drawn vehicles for their supplies. I remember one place where we stayed, they put the Englishmen in a prison, and we were somewhere around twenty to a room, which normally held four. We did have some food there – a kind of soup and a bit of old ryebread. We stayed there just one night. The next day we were off again, and we marched on until we got somewhere near the centre of Belgium, and here we were stopped.

Early next morning we were put on a train, a goods train – forty prisoners to one cattle truck. We went through Belgium on to Trier which is just inside Germany. Here we were unloaded and marched up the hill from the station to a camp of the German Air Force. As we marched up the hill some women and children spat at us while others threw stones and sticks at us; this was a terrible ordeal.

At this camp we were housed outside some huts which were cordoned off. We had to form a queue and we went through the German cookhouse and those of us who had soup-tins or some vessel to hold soup were given a ladleful of soup. At the time I thought this soup very good – I don't know what I would think of it today. We were so hungry that when we had gobbled up our soup we used to join the back of the queue and come for more and we kept this going until the Germans ran out of supplies. We remained at this camp for about three days and then away we went on the notorious train journey.

CHAPTER TWO

POLAND

It was now 13th June, 1940, and we made this train journey from Trier to a very large town in Poland, Poznan. In all it took five days and we were allowed out once a day.

In the very short period that we were allowed out we had to relieve ourselves, we had to get water, and once again a fifth of a loaf. If you can imagine sixty men in a goods wagon, and I am not talking now of a cattle truck, but a goods wagon, there were only four small lights in each corner of the wagon, and from the cracks in the floor and a few cracks in the sides entered all the air we had. So if anyone wanted to relieve himself in any way he just had to. We had no control over our organs because of the vile food we had had; the water and our uncleanliness was absolutely terrible. Before we reached Poznan each of us could put our hands inside our shirts and bring out wads of lice; if you have never seen lice I will give you some idea of what they are like. They are small white insects, about the size of a large grass seed. They live on the human body and actually eat their way into your flesh, and I am told by people who have made a study of lice that many humans carry these lice under the skin in the form of pouches, chiefly under the eyes, and when the system becomes low, then these germs or whatever you like to call them come from the skin and they breed. Later this was also told to me by a German officer when he came into our camp at Fort Rauch in Poznan to give us a lecture about typhus, which was spreading from the Russian front and getting near our camp in Poland.

There was one occasion when we were not allowed out of our goods wagon for over twenty-four hours and you can imagine what our wagon floor was like; it was worse than a pig-sty, and there was nothing we could do about it. Before we got to Poland we pulled into a big siding and we were allowed to wash and we had a loaf of bread and a piece of German *ersatz* butter. I am told that this butter is a by-product of coal.

You can imagine the feeling that we got by even washing our faces, but there were lice in our hair, our arm-pits, our private parts; men who were hairy by nature suffered the most. Apart from the lice not making one in the best of dispositions, the confined space and smell made men irritable. The person who was forced to relieve himself found that he had accidentally soiled his neighbour and this did not help relationships.

But the Germans now gave us this rest-time in the siding. They smartened us up, and then we travelled on to the town of Poznan. It was now 18th June, 1940. They got us out of the train and there was a vehicle in front and then after that came a kind of armoured car and sentries and they marched us Englishmen, about a thousand men, round the town. A loudspeaker on this front car was saying, 'These are the British soldiers who laid down their arms and would not fight for Churchill.' That kept on and on until they marched us down to a camp where the Polish cavalry used to house their horses. It was one of a string of forts which surrounded Poznan in the old days. Also it was the place where many atrocities took place and the bodies of the dead were placed inside the arches and then bricked up.

They placed us in the underground part of this fortress. There was a moat and once we were inside the gate was pulled up, and we were not allowed out; we had our parades down in the moat. The water had been diverted and there was grass at the bottom, and it was here we used to have to assemble to see if we were all in order as far as numbers were concerned.

We had no doctors. In the camp we met some other British prisoners-of-war who had been captured early on in the war. There were two petty-officers from the British submarines *Undine* and *Swordfish*, who told us what the camp was like and what facilities there were, which was next to none. The first thing we had to try and persuade the Germans to do was to get us a doctor for the wounded and there were some bad cases. I remember one man standing on parade next to me. He was a solicitor, and he had got holes in his legs that you could have put two fingers in, and they were alive with lice. He was literally being eaten away and, poor fellow, he did stink. He was so weak and there was nothing we could do about it. The Germans were shown his leg and they took very little notice of him. Later, probably about three or four days, they sent two Polish Medical Corps doctors, and they started looking after us. But the Germans would give them nothing – they could only bring in what they could scrounge. There were many of us who still had shrapnel in us, and that was festering and affecting our nerves, and we were getting headaches and stiff necks from the wounds; my shoulder was very bad by now, it still having shrapnel in it.

The fort was completely round, being about 400 yards in diameter. The ground-floor rooms were divided by great brick arches which also supported the roof which was domed, made of brick and filled in with a sandy earth. No rooms were dry, as water dripped down all the walls. The floor was wet. We were issued with straw to lie on and soon this became wet. There were no Germans inside the fort and we were able to put our straw outside to dry. One day while inspecting the inner chambers, I found a sealed door and after great difficulty and some help from a few other PoWs we opened it and found that it led to the top of the fort where there was a trap-door. I opened this, popped my head out and there was green grass. There were four of us in this little adventure and we found that if we were careful we could lie in the sun without being seen. Also up here there were dandelions and sorrel, which we were able to eat as if it were lettuce.

A lot of our time was spent delousing ourselves, a never-ending task, because the lice eggs developed so quickly. We were not at this fort very long before we were split up – the Navy men going to one camp, the RAF going to another and the Army sent to two camps, one named Schoken and the other named Schubin.

My party was sent to Schubin, there being about four hundred of us of all ranks. This camp was at one time a Polish agricultural school. It had four large sheds where I should think they kept the cattle, with four large ventilator shafts, and, to my pleasure, at the top of one of these shafts, there was a stork's nest. Being a true countryman, this interested me very much, and I spent many hours watching these birds, as I had never seen storks before, but as I travelled around Poland, I saw many.

In this camp the Germans took our particulars and we were issued with Stalag numbers; some men had their Stalag number tattooed on their forearm, others were given a fibre disc with a number printed on it and it had to be worn at all times. My number was 2225. Many of us were unshaven because razor blades were impossible to get and there were not many razors about; a lot of these were shared between members of small groups. I had mine; it was issued at Hillsea Barracks and I always, while in France, carried it in my right-hand breast pocket, with a metal ruler and my Bible in my left. When I was in France an old soldier said that this could quite easily save my life – and I think there was some truth in it. I still use that same razor today, thirty-seven years later. I only shaved once a week and by the time I got to Poland my razor did not cut my bristles, but pulled them out, for we had not seen soap for weeks. Some of the men had all their hair cut off by the Germans, but a corporal of the Queen Victoria Rifles had a pair of nail scissors, and we used to cut each other's hair.

As many men were without footwear, the Germans one day paraded us to change what footwear we had for clogs. Now I had made friends with a Polish worker who spoke fair English and he said, 'Do not go on parade with your boots tomorrow, otherwise the Germans will take them and give you clogs.' He had brought a cartload of clogs into the camp. My boots were new just before we started the retreat and I had got a French shoemaker to put nails on them, where there were no heel-tips or toe-tips, and as we marched through France and Belgium I used to pick up the worn heel-tips and toe-tips from the road and put them in my pocket to replace my nails, and thus kept my boots in fairly good condition. Clogs were terrible to wear, not being flexible; men had terrible blisters, which grew into great raw pieces of flesh and they bled badly. It took a long long time for men's feet to get hard enough to use these things with any kind of comfort and there were no socks to put on the feet first.

I lost track of the man at the fort who had the ulcerated leg on the move to this new camp. Quite by accident I bumped into him at the camp just after we arrived, and his leg was terrible, and nothing had been done. I said to him, 'Will you let me help you,' and he said, 'I will let you do anything; you can cut the damn thing off if you like.' So I got some stinging nettles – I am a great believer in stinging nettles – and some water. I rubbed the stinging nettles together in this water and made it coloured and I bathed his leg with it. Prior to this I had said to the Polish worker, 'Would you get me a box of matches.' He said, 'It is forbidden,' but after promising to let him have them back in half an hour he agreed.

I searched around the camp; there was a lot of pitch and tar about, on the sides of the wooden buildings. I collected pitch and tar, worked it in my fingers until it was about the size of a pencil. I shaved the hairs away from the wound, made him lie on his side, put a piece of timber in his mouth to bite on, because I was going to hurt him. As a countryman I knew that this treatment could do no harm, but knew that when the hot tar dropped into the wound it would be painful; on the farm, when I was a boy, it was used a lot on horses and cattle. Today they still use a form of tar called Stockholm tar for cuts. As my father used to say, 'It keeps bugs and lice out.' This operation was not easy because the matches did not last very long and it was difficult to melt the tar to drip into the wound, but I did it. It was myself who got burnt fingers for the benefit of my patient. This did do good and the wound started to heal well, but how it finished I shall never know because I was saucy to a guard one day and they put me in jail, an open pen with barbed wire round it. I never saw him again after I came out.

In each of the large wooden buildings in the camp the Germans placed a hundred men, and the whole floor was covered in straw. There was just a gang-way up the centre for men to walk to their places to sleep. Try as we did, we could not get rid of the lice; not only were they on our bodies and our clothes, but now they started to fall into the straw and life was hell. The toilet was a long trench with a series of poles to rest one's backside on. About half-a-dozen men had fallen off and died, because they had dysentry and did not have the strength to get back out. A man with dysentry is a pathetic and terrible sight, and the Germans showed no sympathy; they were real bastards. They could afford to be, for they had conquered nearly all of Europe.

I did three days' sentence in the jail and then they let me out. Our food now consisted of a form of soup and two potatoes cooked in their jackets, but we could not eat the potatoes because they had been partly frozen at some time and were soft and horrible. One day a German officer came to look at our conditions. I asked to speak to him and I explained about the potatoes and the lice and the sick and he told me that we were going to get food from the Swiss Red Cross and that a de-lousing plant was coming in to de-louse us, and soon we were all going away to working camps, but in the meantime Polish hard-tack biscuits were to be issued. These biscuits were about five inches by two and a half; intensely compressed, they had caraway seeds in them and were very hard to break. We had one a day, but they certainly helped to fill a hole in one's stomach. Six of us found a way into the stores where the biscuits were kept. For two nights in succession we raided this larder. The biscuits were packed in wooden cases and the store was below ground level, with no window, just iron bars sealing the room from the outside. To get into this in the orthodox way one had to go down steps and through the door; but there was a small area near the opening where we could hide quite comfortably when it was dark. All we wanted was a hack-saw blade. I asked the Polish worker to get me one and he said no, because if he was found out he would be shot. I said if I found one lying on the ground that would be different. So he agreed to get one and I would pick it up. This was how I was able to cut the bars, and bend them so as to enable the smallest member of the gang to get through. On the third night our small friend was not well enough to pull the bars apart, so I went down to do this job, but the unexpected happened. Two Germans came to the door and caught me, and I was put in jail, which they called Lager X; but we had a fair supply of food and this kept us going for several days. There were several Polish workers in this camp and we traded our signet rings for marks and the Poles used to bring us in odd bits of cheese, jam, and best of all, a kind of bread roll which they called zemmels.

The de-lousing plant came. It was drawn by two horses, had four wheels and was very similar to the gully emptiers which the local councils use to clean the drains on the sides of our roads. Mounted on the vehicle was a large steam-generating plant and the steam then went into a horizontal cylinder. At the back of this there was a door, the same size as the cylinder, which, when closed, was sealed tight by about ten bolts, with big fly nuts which kept the steam in. Timber was used in the fire-box. The vehicle was placed near a shed where you stripped. You were given a large sack and into this you put all your clothes and attached a metal number, so that you knew which was yours when it came out. A work party was formed. They collected your bag and placed it in the steam oven. This might sound a simple operation, but it was not. The first mistake which we made was that the clothes were packed too tight into the bags, and the next that there were too many bags in the oven. The steam could not get through, so the lice were not killed. Some of the numbers came off, and it was difficult to sort the clothes out. The outside of the steam chamber had no insulating jacket to stop the cold air getting on to the outside, thus allowing the temperature of the steam inside to drop, and this meant that the clothes came out sodden, and so we had to put the wet clothes back on and to dry them out on our bodies. While the clothes were in the oven we had a cold shower and tried to use the soap which was issued, being nothing more than fine clay in tablet form. I still have one of these as a souvenir. How on earth we never died from pneumonia I shall never know, because we had been damn cold. This de-lousing was a sheer waste of energy we could ill afford. All it did was to give the lice a bath.

From Schubin, I was sent to a small camp on the outskirts of Poznan, with twenty other men, and, being senior NCO, I found myself in charge of this small working party, going out each day to a small farm about five to six miles away. We marched half the way and then two wagons drawn by horses would take us the rest. This was not a pleasant journey as we passed many Jewish women wearing the yellow Star of David, which was sewn on to their clothes. The young and the old were all working in clogs with no socks, making and repairing roads, and they used to say to us, 'Good Mr. Churchill, good England.' This made you proud to be an Englishman. This farm belonged to a Polishman and we went there to pull rhubarb. We only had two guards with us and one spoke some English. One day I said to him, 'If you sit near us you will get lice, but if you make arrangements with the farmer for three of us each day to light the big copper and wash our clothes and de-louse ourselves, it would be good for you.' He did that.

It was now July, 1940; it was very hot, and our clothes dried quickly, but the big problem was to kill the lice and their eggs in the seams of our trousers and battledress blouses. I found the answer; we would take off our trousers, get some warm wood ashes from the boiler fire, open the seams of the trousers and sprinkle the hot ash – then brush it out with a small brush that we made from twigs; after about fourteen days we were all clean.

This work only lasted for the rhubarb season – about a month – and then we were sent to Fort Rauch just on the outskirts of Poznan. This was occupied by British prisoners-of-war. Just a few days after our arrival more PoWs arrived and this brought the number up to a thousand. I stayed in this camp until about September, and this was a very exciting time for me.

My first job was to take a working party out to the railway siding, accompanied, of course, by the German guards, and we had to unload a railway truck of potatoes, which was to be our ration for quite a while. But that was not to be. We loaded these potatoes into a cart drawn by two Polish horses, then had to unload them into a cellar. Fort Rauch was at one time used by the Polish cavalry. The horses were stabled on the ground level, and above them the soldiers were accommodated. There were lecture rooms, and a corridor all the way round with only one entrance, so you could either turn right or left to go to your room, and the same applied to the floor above. Beneath the ground floor there were cellars and it was in one of these that potatoes were stored. The centre of the fort was clear. There was a gravel pathway all the way round and in the centre it was grass. There was only one entrance into the camp and that was by a great door, or rather two great doors, and so in the evening, after you had been on parade for your numbers to be checked, the door was closed and you saw nobody then until six o'clock in the morning, when you were on parade again. We got the first load of potatoes in and within a month they had all gone – stolen by British boys. They used to take them and cook them in their jackets in the old stoves in their rooms. When the cook complained to the Camp Commandant that there were no more potatoes, he went really mad.

He came to me and accused me of allowing the potatoes

to go out. So he said to me that from now onwards I would be in charge of the potatoes. 'It will be your responsibility to make sure you issue the correct amount to the cookhouse so that your men have always got their ration. You will be known as *Der Kartoffel König* and you will be subjected to great discipline and furthermore you will make up from this new ration of potatoes that you are about to receive the deficiency in the last load.' So here I was with a great problem. Everyone was still hungry, but we were not going to get our full ration of potatoes. We had to do some hard thinking. The next load that we had to collect was from the railway station. We went down with a German guard and one of those two-ton wood-burning Opels. When I say wood-burning, I mean they had a gas generating plant on the lorry instead of using petrol. There were several goods wagons filled with potatoes at this railway siding and from one of them we filled our lorry. We took it to the fort and unloaded it. On the way back the lorry broke down and they had to get another one, and this one took us to the station yard and we unloaded potatoes from another wagon, so we had one extra two-ton lorry filled with potatoes. These were taken to our camp and unloaded. Some people might ask how this was possible. It was quite simple. The German corporal in charge was about sixty, and nearly always drunk on Schnapps. I said to one of our gang, 'When we get near to the goods wagon and the truck driver starts to back against it we will guide him on to a different load.' And this is what we did, for there were two German trucks unloading our potatoes and the other one emptied the original truck, and nobody found out that we had an additional two tons of potatoes. That made up for what was stolen. This potato job was not easy – it had many difficulties. I had to detail a party every day, from each room in turn, to peel potatoes for the next day, and a thousand men to peel spuds for is quite an undertaking.

While out working on the potato wagons, I made friends with a Polishman, and I asked him if he could get a radio into our camp. He used to come to our camp and do carpentry and fitting up pipes in the cookhouse, and seeing to water. He said he would try, and he came one day and gave a friend of mine a radio set. He brought it to our room where there were twelve of us. We were all sergeants and staff sergeants and each night we used to listen in to the news and take notes of interesting things we heard. We used to give the Commander of each room a brief outline of what was happening all over the world, but we found that news got so distorted that we had to do this listening on a very correct basis. That meant finding somebody who could do shorthand, and we found a corporal from a Scottish regiment. We made up a committee of three and the man really responsible for the news travelling through many camps in Poland was a man named Sgt. Ted Oborne; I think he was something to do with the Post Office. Nevertheless, he did work in the Post Office in Poznan dealing with all the mail that came from England, because Poznan was the centre of British prisoners-of-war at this particular time. He would sort the mail from England into various camps and would open the odd letter and stick a news item in. So Ted was the news supplier, and what a wonderful job he did. No news ever got into German hands – not on one occasion did any of our news letters get captured by anybody associated with the Germans and this certainly brightened up the lives of our boys. At least we knew what was going on. In our camp I used to lecture twice a week on everything about the war. I remember describing the jeep – how all the Americans used to travel by jeep and what it could do, the kind of gun and the number of personnel it could carry.

One day, late in August, myself and fifty other ranks were sent to the railway sidings and put into goods wagons and we were shipped off by rail to a camp right on the edge of the River Vistula. Also on this train were another fifty British prisoners-of-war. When we arrived at this camp I had a shock because the fifty that I had in my camp were clean, but the others were dirty – with lice to a very great extent. We found that they had been sent from Schoken to another small working camp and had not had very fair treatment –

29

certainly not living in the conditions that we had been living in recently. This camp that we were about to take over was a Polish farmhouse. It had three rooms and there were two barns – one we used for a cookhouse and the other one for stores, and fuel for the coppers. The farmhouse had one long room, one medium sized room and one very small room and we hundred men fitted in the three rooms to the best of our ability. It was difficult because there was no gangway to go in by – everybody had to go up the passageway to the right for one room – left for another room and straight on for the third room. We had no beds or anything like that – all we had was straw again. This was all right while the weather was good but it soon became dirty.

We were set to work to make a roadway in the forest and to get into the forest we had about an hour's march there and an hour's march back. We had to use and make concrete and one of the things that used to happen after we had done a day's work was that the tools used to be thrown into the concrete, so when we went to work the next day we were probably one shovel or one pick short. This didn't please the Jerries very much. Once I remember a corporal from the Gloucesters threw a wheelbarrow down the bank where the concrete was and that is where the wheelbarrow is today I suppose. So that was one wheelbarrow less and one part of the road which took a bit longer to make.

The food in this camp was terrible – nothing but barley, barley, barley. That is just the ordinary barley that you would feed cattle on – put in a copper and boiled until it was something like a porridge and once or twice a week we would get some beetroot to throw in, and once a week some kind of meat. One way that I used to get protein into our food was to trap any kind of bird that hung around our camp and this is how it was done. I made a frame from wood that we brought back from the forest. Then I got odd bits of string and made a net. This I fixed to the frame which was about three feet by four feet. I laid it on the ground, then put a stick to hold it at an angle of about 25°. On the stick tie some string; put some grains of barley on the ground, then take the string and hide. When there are birds under the net, pull the string and they are caught in the net. I then broke their necks, skinned and gutted them and when they were three or four days old put them in the barley to cook. This operation I continued for quite a while. To drink they used to supply us with *ersatz* coffee which was made from burnt rye and also German tea which was made from wild mint and sage and various wild herbs.

This camp was under the control of Poznan and occasionally we used to get the German Sergeant-Major come up and see us. He was known as 'The Bull'.

October came and it started to get really cold and we still had only got the clothes we were captured in. Then the snows came and we couldn't work or go out or do anything. We had no food, or very little – the barley was getting short. In charge of us was a corporal, and I said to him one day, 'When the Sergeant-Major comes, will you allow me to speak to him.' He said he would and when the 'Bull' came over I said, 'We have no clothes, the men have no rags round their feet and we can't work; we are going to have a lot of trouble in this camp. We shall have men die from the cold. Can you get us some overcoats.' And he did. But he did not get them until November when the snow was on the ground and it was jolly cold. And for our hundred men we had twelve overcoats in the first issue – twelve Polish cavalry overcoats. They were wonderful coats because not only did they cover the soldier but they covered part of the horse as well, but try and divide twelve coats up between a hundred men who had no coats; it is like the good Lord feeding the five thousand. The next week came about two dozen square cloths which we had to use as socks. They were equally difficult to divide up. The next week there came somewhere between forty and fifty greatcoats – all Polish. So we had now about two-thirds of the camp clothed in greatcoats – but we were still very short of foot-rags. All during this time we had our problem with lice. I separated the men from my camp from the other ones and they took their shirts off and hung them on the barbed wire. The boys used to go de-licing on the barbed wire with bits of stick from the cookhouse. These of course would be hot and they would singe the shirt and singe the lice. It was only for a very short period while the sun was out that you could do this and when the sun went down about 2 p.m. you wished that you had more than one shirt.

December came and the snows and the frost. Luckily we had all got greatcoats by now, but the food was very scarce, the difficulty being transportation, because the River Vistula was beginning to freeze. Our corporal wasn't too difficult a man to get along with and I said to him one day that we had had no meat for such a long time, 'Can we go up to the butchers and get meat?'

When I talk of meat ration, it means that we had about one ounce of meat per man per week, and I dearly wanted to get into that slaughter-house for I was sure that I should be able to pinch something.

He said, 'You must make an application to Poznan and if they say yes, then you can go along with a guard and bring meat down to the cookhouse.' After about fourteen days we got this permission and myself and a German used to go to the slaughterhouse and bring back our ration. I got on very well with the butcher. One day he pushed a pig's liver inside my battledress and that was very good indeed, but my body was very messy with blood. All the German wanted was enough for himself and three guards, and the rest I took into our house and I cut it up into equal parts – some for the small room, some for the middle room and some for the big room; that was cut up again and then the men had to draw lots. After they had had their meat their number was taken so that when I got more they wouldn't have a second helping and so each man had meat in his turn as it was available. I went up three times a week for about one month. I had pig's chitterlings, pig's feet, ears, tongues and pig sausage. We did quite well, but the standard of living and eating was very low, and the Germans were always rubbing it in that they had control of the whole of Europe and we should be thankful for what we got. At this time the Germans did not recognize the Geneva Convention; they were, as you might say, 'on top of the world'.

By this time winter was truly upon us. I had been able to get the German guard to let me have my boots and three other men's boots repaired by the Polish shoemaker in the village. This was country where a vast extent of forestry was carried out and in the breaks of the forest big plantations of sugar beet were grown.

It was interesting to see the number of deer and hares that there were. I had never seen deer to this extent. Polish winters are extremely severe. The sun rises in the morning and by midday it is going down and during that period it has melted the snow on the roofs and so there is a constant trickle falling down the already existing icicles and it is nothing to see icicles here two and three feet in width, where the sun has come out only long enough to melt some snow for it to drip, drip, drip. The snow is deep also. It is impossible for horses to draw a vehicle along the road; they have to revert to sledges.

Now we had run out of bread and had had no bread for two days. It left me no alternative but to plead with the German in charge of our camp to allow me to cross over the Vistula with a guard and try and scrounge some flour from somebody; but he wouldn't hear of it, so we went two more days without any bread, and as it was we had only been having one fifth of a loaf. That is a small tin loaf in English size, which you can eat in one meal quite easily. The bread situation got quite serious and I had to do something. I said to the corporal, 'Would you let a guard come with me and I will cross the Vistula, and go and see if I can get somebody to let the Germans have a hundredweight of flour on credit. Then our cook can make dumplings or something.' After some yesses and noes and excuses, he agreed to come with me.

The Vistula had frozen and the ice-packs stood up two or three feet where the floes of ice had floated down and congregated in certain spots. The wind blew from the steppes of Russia, right down through Poland and all along the Vistula. The wind and snow were so bad that when we started to cross the river the wind got into our cavalry coats which were like big tents on us, and they just blew us away from each other. I lost the guard and I shouted and shouted but he couldn't hear me. Suddenly I heard him shouting to me. We got together again and we crossed the Vistula and got into a big town. I think it was called Woslavik, but I am not sure. But we went into the town and I had a great reception. The first shop we went into was the tobacco shop and they had some nice cigarettes in there, very similar to our Virginia. I think they were called Tonga and I had two hundred given me and the German had fifty for himself, and we didn't have to pay for them. From this shop he told us where the bakery was and we went to the bakery. There were some people kneading bread, and I explained to them who I was and I came away from there with half a hundredweight of flour, some currants, some sultanas and some lard, and about forty to fifty eggs. In all I had just over one hundredweight to carry, and I had to carry this approximately three miles in this terrible snow-storm and strong wind back across the Vistula, having to keep clear of the small icebergs. It was slippery, and I carried all these things back to within about half a mile from the camp when I slipped and broke a lot of eggs. How tired I was – no home to come back to, no nice warm food and no one to take care of me. All I had was some louse-ridden straw. How I hated those bastard Germans.

The next day I went to the slaughter-house again and I got blood sausage, chitterlings, and some pigs' trotters and tails and some liver, and came back into the rooms for it to be divided up. It was a difficult job to divide small amounts of food between a hundred men. However, half a hundredweight of flour was something, but there was not a lot of lard, so I persuaded the German officer in charge to let me go over again with two of his guards and two of my room mates, so that we could get some more food over. We went again and each of us carried half a hundredweight of flour, and some potato flour also and a form of meat cube which we made into a kind of gravy. What with the first amount of

34

food we got and now this, it made us quite a respectable meal for a couple of days.

During this time several of our boys got frost-bite in their ears and toes, and the Polish doctor in the village took one fellow's toes off. The blisters would break and they had terrible ears and feet.

At last the snow ceased and it was possible for people and vehicles to move about, so the Commandant of Poznan sent vehicles out to collect us because we were just about at the end of our tether. We were beginning to get extremely ill, and they took us now to another camp called Kernverk, another of the ring of forts round Poznan.

Here in Poznan I saw some terrible things. It seemed that members of the Nazi party were nothing more than wild beasts. I myself witnessed a few examples of the sort of humiliation that the Poles had to endure. I remember one day that a coal cart was going up a street in Poznan, when a large piece of coal fell off the back of it. An old Polish woman went out and picked it up and then ran after the cart calling the driver to stop. A Nazi NCO who was passing shouted to the driver to stop, took his whip from him, and thrashed the old lady until she collapsed. There was one other incident that occurred not long after we had arrived, in the camp. This made me realize the cold-bloodedness and ruthlessness of the Germans. From some houses near the camp three young Jews were publicly hanged. We were deliberately exercised where we could not fail to see the whole procedure. The guards told us that one of the three was only sixteen and the others were in their early twenties. We asked what their crime was. 'Sabotage,' was the reply. They did not expect us to believe them and half smiled as they answered. It was their stock answer to such foolish queries.

I heard much of the unspeakable atrocities practised by the Germans and in my four and a half years of captivity I saw many horrible things, but somehow the memory of those Jewish boys swinging in the breeze is one that will remain with me until I die.

I did not remain very long at Poznan and was soon off to

another small working camp on the Vistula, it now being early spring, 1941. Here we were sent to help a party of Polish engineers repairing a bridge over the Vistula which the Poles had blown up during the German invasion. The discipline was lax on this working party and I sometimes managed to slip away to talk to an American Pole who was an engineer. He brought me food each day and it was always a sandwich of some sort. Sometimes it was the fat of goose entrails or goose potted meat or pig fat and all these had onions in. I remember these to this day – they were extremely tasty and I enjoyed them very much indeed. But I was not allowed to share because if I or any other members of the working party had been caught eating any part of this, the Pole would have been in dire trouble. The main reason I had this extra food given to me was to help me get fit for my first escape. The engineer brought me a lumber-jacket and a balaclava. I did not speak with my friend every day because he was going to help me and he was gathering information and we did not want anyone to guess our relationship. The Poles always did their very best to help us. They were very kind to all PoWs as far as they could be, but their life was a very miserable one.

It was now spring, just before the Germans attacked Russia. My friend thought I should try to get into the corridor between Poland and Russia and make for a place which I think was called Plock, but I am not sure. I was to travel by road, getting rides with Polish farmers until I got to a railway junction, but I do not remember the name of this even. My friend had written something on a piece of paper which I had to show to any Polish person whom I thought might be of assistance to me. This worked well and I travelled a long way following the course of the Vistula and I arrived at this railway junction, and there I had to see if I could find a goods truck going east for I had been given certain names to look for. One thing that you must have when escaping is a photographic mind and a good memory. Fortunately I had both. I got captured here by a funny-looking weasel-eyed German policeman and I pretended to be deaf and dumb. If the policeman had had a grain more sense he might have understood what my gesticulation meant and let me go, but he had no comprehension of any kind and of course I had no papers, so my brief freedom came to an end. I realize now that I must have been damn daft to have gone. It showed me how ignorant of current affairs I was and how vast a project this was, but I learnt a lot.

I got away by going to the bridge-building site, collecting my escape kit, going to a pre-arranged site and waiting for a haulage contractor to pick me up and get me on my way. This part was well planned and executed.

These men had friends all along the way and if it was safe they would pass me on. If not I would stay at a small farm. The men had to travel to certain collecting centres where everything in the way of food was taken for the Germans to re-distribute and so it was quite a meeting place at times. The country was very flat with a sandy soil and vast acres of sugar beet. There were large flocks of geese and where we would have a shepherd in the British Isles, the Poles had geese-minders.

I remember staying one night at a very small farm. The farmer's main work was on one of these sugar beet areas, but he kept a cow and calf, a yearling beast fattening for the butcher, about four goats and about half-a-dozen sheep and fifteen to twenty hens. The outbuildings for the cattle were of a low standard. The goats and chickens lived in the farm-house with the farmer, his wife and daughter.

Their clothes were in bad shape, but I did see three sheep-skin coats that had been home-dressed and made into great-coats. Their boots were strong leather high-leg boots, but there were also clogs. Headgear looked as if they had been made from lambskin. If I understood them properly from their gesticulations, they never took their clothes off in the winter because it was so cold. I can appreciate their feeling of cold for I had been through it. They explained that the weather was so bad sometimes that they could not leave their 'house'.

This 'house' was a long wooden shed with a heavy

timbered roof, and a kind of felt on top and then timber again. Four windows, and there were wooden shutters that could be drawn across on the outside. Inside there was a large cylindrical oven. I should think that this was about ten feet long and about three feet in diameter. There were lots of clothes and blankets on top on a kind of square frame. On top of this the man slept, and the other two slept near the side. The building would be about thirty feet long and about twenty feet wide and it housed everything including the goats and chickens, but it was warm. These people made their own bread from whole wheat and rye corn, which they ground themselves. There were great earthenware jars filled with pig fat which they used as butter, and there were lots of onions strung up. Also there was half a side of a very large pig which had been cured so hard that they had to soak it before they could cook it. There were also jars of goose fat; some of it had had onions cooked in it, and I liked this. The other goose fat they used to rub on their hands and feet. Truly this was a most interesting place and they did me well. I only stayed here one night and I was off again.

After I was captured, the German police took me to the police station and here I was interviewed by the Gestapo. I told them I was a British prisoner-of-war Stalag 21D No. 2225, and that I had escaped from my working party about six miles out of Poznan. He asked me where I got my lumber-jacket from. I told him that I had stolen it and he wanted to know where. He kept asking me questions and I said I could not answer them because the Geneva Convention stated that I was not obliged to. All I was obliged to do was to give my Army rank and number – no more than that. But I went on to explain that most of all, I could not understand his English. This annoyed him greatly, and he then hit me so hard that he knocked me across the room and cut my eye. He stood me up and said, 'What did you say,' and I told him that I could not understand him. So he hit me again and knocked me down and then stamped out of the room, leaving me to the old weasel-faced policeman, who put me into a cell where I remained for six days on bread and water.

I was sent back to Poznan, accompanied by a German guard and I served another seven days on bread and water, but I never answered the questions about where I got my lumber-jacket from and where I got my other bits and pieces for my escape from, or who helped me.

From this time my story jumps two years until I found myself in a camp in Bavaria. Strange as it may sound, I have no recollection of what happened during that period. All I can recall is that in the spring of 1942 I found myself in Camp 383.

CHAPTER THREE

CAMP 383

383 WAS a prisoner-of-war camp situated high up in the Bavarian hills on the edge of a great pine forest, approximately 80 kilometres from Nürnberg, 150 kilometres from Munich, 48 kilometres from Regensburg and 52 kilometres from Neumarkt.

Before prisoners-of-war came to Camp 383 it was part of a German military training camp for tanks and cavalry. The training area covered about twenty miles by fifteen. About two miles from its southern border, the Germans wired off an area of small huts, and in these they placed fourteen men per hut. Parsberg was the nearest railway station to it, being about fifteen kilometres distance away, and to get to this station was a very windy route with great woods all the way down. Not far from our camp, about a mile, there was another camp. This was a French prisoner-of-war camp, and not far from that camp, about a mile, there was a small farm being part of the village of Hohenfels.

The camp was controlled by the Germans from the outside and patrols were sent in to keep an eye on things day and night. Later the patrols were increased by thirty NCOs, owing to the activities of about sixty British prisoners-of-war who continually tried to escape. Great credit must be given to various British organizing parties who attended to the welfare of the camp. Also I cannot give enough praise to the International Red Cross and YMCA who cared for our food, medical care, amusements, etc. They did a grand job and without their help many of us would not be alive today. The great man of the camp was Major Brook-Moore, Royal Army Medical Corps, AIF, who cared for our sick and carried out many operations under extreme difficulties. He was a great man. Also SQMS MacKenzie must be given a word of praise, for he was our 'Man of Confidence' and did a lot of really good and hard work for all of us.

We had two theatres, one where we could always see a first-class play and the other where only variety shows were put on. There were two dance bands, accordion band, military band, symphony orchestra, a Spanish band and a mouth-organ band. Twice a week dances were held; the nearest approach to women were men who used to dress up as girls, and they were really very good indeed.

Before the British arrived there was no recreation of any sort. The PoWs made this camp the best in Germany.

The gymnasium was always packed and apart from that there were several groups of PT. Much football, rugby, hockey and Australian-rule football was played and cricket was always exciting in the season, especially when the Aussies played the English for the Ashes. Baseball, an all-year-round sport, was well patronized. When the fire-pond froze ice-skating took place with skates that the boys had acquired by blackmarket with the Germans and in the summer we could get an occasional swim providing the Huns never caught us.

The busiest part of the camp was the college. Here very many subjects were taken and I should say that at least one fifth of the camp was studying something. The concert halls and gym and college were disused stables and the interiors were built up and separated by the wooden boxes that the bulk Red Cross food came in, which were taken to pieces. There was a very large sports field which held a football and hockey pitch. One could always see some game being played and also if one watched faces carefully one could pick out the escapers getting into training, walking around the field. From the sports field many escapes were attempted; some were temporarily successful and some not.

Archie McGee and his little gang were very clever. One of their attempts was when they took the bedboards from their bunks and made a hole on the ground big enough for a man to get inside. When this was big enough, a man would get in; they would place the bedboards on top of the hole, put the turves back and the man would stay there until it was dark. It is very difficult to imagine how long it is to wait from six o'clock in the evening when the sports field closed, in hiding until perhaps eight o'clock at night, in the early spring, before one can get out from one's cramped position, lift the boards and see who is around, listen to hear where the German guard and his dog are, watch for the searchlights which were played around and decide what kind of camouflage one must have to crawl on the ground to get near the wire before one cuts it. Fortunately, in the beginning, when this form of escape was put into operation there were only two watch-towers and the beams of the lights did not reach the centre of the field. It was in the centre of the field that the hole was dug, approximately twenty feet inside the trip wire. The trip wire was an electric fence, a single strand from which we would get a nasty shock if we touched it. A warning was given if we got near the wire and the Germans would then automatically shoot if their warning was not heeded, and this was a fact, and it did happen once.

Now all this digging was very complicated because the earth had to be moved, so one had to find means of transporting it from the sports field, which, as I have said, was very large. It meant working under the eyes of the Germans in the watch-towers and the German guards whom we called

41

'Snoops', who used to come into the camp and walk round and see what we were doing. So this is the kind of picture one would see – Archie and his men would take with them to the sports field bedboards and blankets, spade and pick, and they would dig. They would then get their earth-removing plant working. This comprised Red Cross boxes, empty cardboard cartons, large pockets of greatcoats, or anything which would carry earth without being observed by the Germans. The great difficulty of this was that there was a lot of chalk and also a lot of red sandstone in places, so we were always having to be very careful that we got no mud or clay on us, which would draw the attention of the guards to our activities. The next thing was where to place the earth. To dig a hole about three feet square and four feet deep is no mean exercise to carry out under the noses of the Germans.

With a pair of stolen wire cutters we cut a hole in the wire; and away the escaper would run, leaving his wire cutters hidden at a specified place. He had approximately three hundred yards to go before he could get into the cover of some shrubs which led into the wood, but the great difficulty was that the outside of the sports field was controlled by German police and military police with their Alsatian dogs.

There were two sets of fifteen strands of barbed wire ten feet high, with a coiled set in between them. So after the first part of the wire had been cut, the coiled wire had to be bashed down, so that the next set of wire strands were accessible. When wire is cut in the stillness of the night it sounds as if all the world could hear it. The amazing thing was that the Germans never heard us cut the wire otherwise we would probably have been dead. One other difficulty was that the strain on the wire was such that every time you cut it, it would spring back and coil around you. There was also another problem. Before we got to this stage we had all our goods and chattels to take to a hiding place, ready for our survival after escape, including our rations which were made into a form of biscuit, which comprised a variety of other biscuits from our food parcels. These were pulverized and mixed with margarine and currants and baked in our home-made ovens. These were made from tins that had contained items in our Red Cross parcels. The biscuits were horrible and went mouldy. Another point one must realize is that when one has been cramped down in a hole for about four hours or more, one's circulation has gone, one is cold, and of course one's brain doesn't work very well. It takes quite a while to get accustomed to the stillness and darkness and to the various shadows one sees as the clouds cross the moon's path.

The first eleven months in this camp I studied German at the school, but I had already started to learn German when I was in Poland. Before I was able to take my place in the class, I was interviewed by Dr. Elguther, who was a German Jew who had to flee Germany during the persecution in 1933. He escaped to Palestine and when the Palestinian Army was formed he joined it, was captured at Crete and so found his way to Stalag 383.

I found his A Class was too far advanced for me so I asked if I might join Class B, which was being conducted by a lieutenant from the German Army who had come back from Russia. The Professor introduced me to the lieutenant and he agreed to take me. I got on very well and after a while I asked if I could write essays as homework. He agreed, provided my essays were no more than four hundred words per evening and that he could read my essays only twice a week. And so I started my essays on travels from one village to another and what I should meet on the way and the type of country and the kind of birds I should see, and the fruit and what transportation there was. That was my first essay. The next I wrote about town life, and what there was in the towns and the kind of people who were there. My imagination, of course, was very wrong, but it was an essay and it was corrected. My next essay was about Regensburg and the Danube and what kind of river boats there were and the small villages along the Danube. After this I came back and dealt with the towns again and said that I had been for a tour of one of the big towns, that I had been to a theatre and I had seen a newsreel and that I had gone to a café. Of course this was an imaginary story, and when the officer corrected it he asked me if I had anything in particular in mind and why I wrote this type of essay, and I said, 'Well, it is very obvious that perhaps one day I might be able to make an excursion and I would need this kind of information that I have been writing about.' The lieutenant corrected my essays and he filled in some necessary details; that coupons were needed to go to a restaurant and there was only a certain type of food you could eat in a restaurant, that you could only have *ersatz* coffee in a restaurant and there were no barbers. So that answered some of my questions.

My next essay was an imaginary train journey. How I bought my ticket; what kind of questions would be asked when I went to the kiosk for my necessary papers; did I have to have a travel visa or certificate to show my work as well as a travel ticket, and where did one find the time-tables. I gave this to the officer for correction and once more he answered my questions, and after that he did give me quite a lot of advice. I settled down to study German properly and caused no more embarrassment to the officer. I worked very hard indeed. I spoke to Dr. Elguther and asked him if we could arrange to have conversations together in colloquial German, and he agreed that every other day we should walk round the sports field and do one complete tour, no more, and we would talk in colloquial German, so that I would be able to face minor difficulties without any complications.

My next mission was to meet a French soldier named Wally Whitehead. He was a Scotsman who had married a French girl and they were living in Paris when the war broke out. He was a dress designer and came to our camp with four other men to do odd jobs which British officers were not allowed to do under the Geneva Convention. I contacted him because he had a German friend who would help me with various items I required, when I came to put my essays to a practical use.

Wally Whitehead duly came into the camp, along with the

44

German guard, an under-officer by the name of Karl Schneider. We met and it was agreed that Schneider would help me because he was French and not German to his way of thinking, having been conscripted into the German Army. His father was German and his mother was French, but he had lived near Strasbourg, his people owning a guest house not far away, so all his sympathies were with the French and British and he was to help me to a great extent.

CHAPTER FOUR

TUNNELLING

I WENT to work on a tunnel, having been asked by a friend if I would make the team up as one had met with an accident. This tunnel was about ten feet beneath the surface and was planned to run about eighty feet in length. Despite being able to work only at night when the electric current was on, we finished more than half our work in six weeks and would have been even quicker but for the handicap of wet mud. None of us could find where this water was coming from. One night about June, Alan Morrison descended the ten-foot shaft entrance and crawled part of the way along the tunnel and started to work. Suddenly there was a terrific slide of earth from the walls, and the tunnel collapsed and buried him. Fortunately he was only about seven-eighths buried and with a lot of difficulty we managed to get him out. We cleared the debris and after stealing more timber from various places, we shored this fallen part of the roof up and started to work again. When we got about six feet further in I found what the trouble was. Morrison and I were working together, when I ran my spade against something metal-like at the side of the tunnel and I called Alan back to me and we dug out a four-inch water main. Now we dug along for about six feet hoping that this would clear away and go into a different direction, but this was not to be. So we climbed back up to the hut and had a consultation and decided that it was necessary to go out on a wood-collecting party and bring in some timber. These wood-working parties were allowed only once a month per hut and only two people from each hut were to go out into the area where timber-felling was taking place and to bring in small pieces of timber. The pieces of timber that we managed to bring in were about three inches in diameter and we sawed them up under the supervision of the Germans, into about three foot lengths. We really had a load when we got back because there was a great necessity to have timber to shore the walls and the pipes.

Alan and I went down and we used this timber to save the tunnel, or tried to. Now the big question was, where did this pipe go and what was it supposed to do? There were German civilians working on the fire-pond because the Swedish Red Cross had been to inspect our camp and had reported to Geneva that there was no fire-pond and the Germans were now forced to fulfil this request. While this work was going on I talked to various workmen on the site and at last I found that the water was going to be pumped in from the direction of our hut, so we had a conference and all of us agreed that this water would pass through the pipe which was exposed in our tunnel. We had to get more timber because we were frightened that when they started to pump the water from the main water supply into this fire-pond, it would set up a vibration in the early stages and probably fracture the pipe. Undaunted by Alan's mishap, we carried on. As this seeping of water was making work so hard it was difficult to pull the sledge backward and forward as we moved the soil away from the face of the tunnel, because the rope, made of plaited Red Cross string from Red Cross parcels, became clayed up and slippery and also the weight of the small sledge which held about twenty pounds of earth at a time cut tracks in the base of the tunnel. It was suggested that we made a concrete track, so that the sledge could run over it to the shaft. This meant that we had to concrete from the face to the end of the shaft and it gave us a nice firm base to stand on so that we could lift the earth from the shaft to the tunnel up to the floor of our hut. This was agreed. We went on a 'borrowing' mission again. This time it was to the fire-pond. We got the Germans busy while one of us 'borrowed' a sack of cement. This was a very funny incident. Our pal took a sack of cement, and got about twenty yards away when one of the workmen spotted him. He started shouting; then four of the workmen started running after him. We shouted to our pal to run. Just as he got to a row of huts he bumped into two German soldiers so they took up the hunt. Into a hut dived our pal. An occupant of the hut held the sack while he jumped out of the window, then he took the sack, crawled between two huts and then did the same. Meanwhile the rest of us were running in and out and causing the Germans a lot of hindrance. By this time many other British boys saw what was going on and joined in the fun and so we got our bag of cement. At night we took sand from the fire-pond, from the fire boxes and anywhere we could find sand and we made our concrete run. After working several more days we ran into trouble. We had another fall of earth and it seemed as though this tunnel was doomed. The last shift came up at four o'clock in the morning and everything was okay. At two o'clock in the afternoon the British senior camp policeman came and woke me up as I was resting prior to going down for my four-hour shift. He asked me if I had a tunnel going in the camp and I asked, 'Why?' and he replied, 'Well, you had better come and put your deep sea diving suit on because it is full of water.' Off I went and when I got there many of the gang were there with long faces – for we had dug about a hundred feet, nearly long enough for the tunnel to be finished and water was oozing out of the ground. Now starts the funny side.

When I got there the water was over the floor of the hut and was oozing out and going over the floor of the next hut. The alarm had been given and there stood the German foreman who had been working on the fire-pond with his hat off watching the water, scratching and shaking his head and trying to work out what had happened. As the water rose so the gardens at back of the hut sank in. These gardens were only about four feet wide and about fourteen feet long. You can guess how disappointed we were although we couldn't help but laugh. One minute there was a garden – the next minute it had completely disappeared. This was not all. Our neighbours in the next hut crowded to the window to see the fun and the darn hut fell down, finishing at an angle of about 40°. By this time all the German Officers had arrived. They asked us what had happened and we said we did not know.

They had the water turned off at the mains. Before the 'snoops' arrived we had destroyed the camouflage of the entrance and one of our boys said it was a pity to leave the spades and tunnelling equipment down there and he was going down to retrieve what he could. Now the shaft was ten feet deep and it was a plucky thing to go down to this depth.

He stripped off and we cut a blanket up and tied the ends together and he sank to the bottom taking the rope of blanket with him so that we could pull him up when he jerked the rope. He retrieved the tunnelling equipment and we pulled him up.

In the centre of the hut was a fire stove that was part of the furniture, but against this we had made up a dummy oven and this was our hide to the entrance of the tunnel. The Germans could hardly believe their eyes when they saw this oven floating about on the floor. The Chief Security Officer was sent for and he came along with other guards, who surrounded the hut and took us for interrogation. He accused us of digging a tunnel. We asked him what right he had to accuse us of digging a tunnel, when other people had been in the hut before us. We understood there had been some Serbians there. Surely they could have dug the tunnel and not us, but perhaps it was not a tunnel. I said to Hauptmann Blumm, 'I think you will find this is a fracture caused by subsidence of ground.' He did not agree with me, and for our pains he stopped all the Red Cross parcels coming into the camp for two weeks. You can imagine we were not very popular. The next day the 'snoops' found the tunnel but they could not prove that we had dug it, so no one went to prison.

The Camp Commandant was very angry and he said that we had got to dig it up and find the reason. They thought that we had broken a pipe while we were tunnelling because they had a plan of the camp showing that they had a water system near this hut of ours. We refused, so they kept the camp on only one-third of water supply. This went on for three days and so much inconvenience was caused to other PoWs that when the German Second-in-Command came around and asked us to dig it up we agreed but only on the condition that we were paid because they had not been able to prove that we had caused the damage. He said that he could not pay us in Lager money* as the Berlin Authorities would want to know why Lager money was required and this would cause a lot of upheaval and this he wanted to avoid. For his sake and ours, instead of paying us in money, he would allow us to have two bottles of beer each per day while we were working. Beer was, at that time, an unheard-of thing, so, taking everything into consideration, we set to work. By working thus it provided us with the means to get necessities for our next tunnel. We dug the tunnel up and found the cause of the flooding. This is what had happened. The Germans, when they built the camp, had taken a two-inch lead off the main supply and had connected it up to the supply to the wash-house about twenty yards away. Instead of joining a two inch to a four inch in a solid way they had drilled a seven-eighths hole in the top of the four inch and put in a U-clamp bolt under which fitted the two-inch flange with its rubber jacket. Instead of the two-inch pipe coming off at right angles they had strained it over to about 15° because the water line was not in line with the wash-house. We fitted a new pipe and that fulfilled our contract – so we 'borrowed' all the timber that the Germans brought in for

*An artificial currency used by the Germans to pay for the labour of British PoWs obliged to work under the terms of the Geneva Convention.

the job, and a spade, and a pick as well. This annoyed the Germans but they could do nothing about it for we explained that it must have been taken for firewood and that there was an error in the checking up of tools, and that we had only agreed to open up the tunnel and not fill it in. So the Germans were beaten and they had to bring in a French working party to finish the job.

Karl Schneider was coming into the camp quite often now. He used to bring the post in and slip away down to my hut to bring me items that I required because I had a plan. The plan was that eight of us were going to dig another tunnel and we were going to come out on the north side of the camp.

This tunnel was to be my project. It was agreed that I would be in complete control and that everybody would obey my instructions right to the last letter and that we were going to start our tunnel from the second hut in on the north side of the camp, being only two huts away from one of the main roads past the camp.

Before we started to dig we had to do a lot of camouflaging and it took time to get this working because it needed the assistance of the Camp Commandant, Col. Aufhammer. I had to wait for an opportunity when he came to the camp to inspect our part to ask him 'a favour'. The huts, which were eight in a line in our particular row, ours being the second one, fell down in contour from their doorsteps to the roadway. There would be about two feet fall, and in a hut area which measured about fourteen to sixteen feet in width, that gave us a fair latitude in which to deposit our waste earth. I had to ask the Commandant for his permission for us to start a vegetable garden as our blood was out of sorts and we were getting spots and we needed more greenstuff. I explained that we had eaten all the dandelions in the camp and there were no more stinging nettles; we had to do something or we would all be down with scurvy. So he said what did I suggest. I suggested that we made the front part of our hut into a garden, growing greenstuff and a few flowers at the back just to make it look nice and bright, and he thought this was a good idea – and thought what a nice tidy lot of Englishmen we were. So we got permission to ask the Red Cross for some seeds which eventually arrived. But before they arrived I had already got some from Karl Schneider. The earth was the greatest problem in tunnelling, where to put it, without having to carry it far. The Colonel had given us permission to make a garden and I had explained to him what we were going to do – level the garden up – put flowers at the back etc., etc. Now we did not make our entrance from our own hut, but from the hut in front of us, Hut No. 1. As we were subject to lots of control, because there were two escapers, myself and Ted Hartman, the Germans came in several times a day to look at us, so it would be senseless making our tunnel start from here. The entrance to the tunnel was made under the first bed, just as we came in from the door, so it meant that the most we had to go was about thirty feet. That would mean we would go under the road which the tanks would go over. There was an old Ammo shed which was delapidated; we would come out close to it and it would give us a good blind to the machine-gun towers. So we started.

It was a difficult job, because first of all we had to cut the floorboards so precisely that they would go back with no obvious cuts that the 'snoops' would notice. We had to start digging in the hut, at night when it was dark. One man at one window at the back and one sitting out by the porchway kept watch for us. It was an extremely difficult job, because once you are past your arm's length it makes your blood run to your head when your head is down in the ground. Our tools were not what they might be – self-made tools, bits of iron, spades or shovels with the handles sawn off which we had stolen or 'organisiert' from the various working parties when they came in.

We got down to the bottom of the shaft. The next job, once you are down, is to start your tunnel, away from your entrance and if one Sunday you are working in your garden and would like some exercise, just try lying on your tummy,

51

digging a hole with poor tools, and after you have dug a shaft go down and dig a tunnel. You will find you will not need any exercise for a month after that.

We got down to the bottom, started digging, and we ran into no difficulties whatsoever, except the lack of food because the Red Cross parcels were not coming in very often. To work on the German food was impossible and if it hadn't been for my friend Karl Schneider, I don't think we could have maintained these efforts because the exhaustion after two hours down there was absolutely intense. After we had driven our tunnel through for about six feet we had to work up a system of carrying the earth from the face to the rear to get it disposed of and this is what I did. I found a sack and laid it on the ground against the face of the tunnel and tied a cord which was made up of string from Red Cross parcels. I would work at the face, put the sack underneath my knees so that the earth fell through my knees on to the sack, and my colleague behind me would pull it away from me.

In the beginning this worked well, myself digging, and the earth falling on to my sack. When the earth was hard against my legs, I would raise my body and Archie McGee would pull the sack away from me, and I would sit down again. At the end of the tunnel others would pull the earth out, and they would then give it to friends lying underneath the hut floor who would give it to others to deposit. So by this method we had men doing the same job the whole time, and each man became a form of specialist. We worked two hours in one shift in the morning and two hours about tea-time. Four hours a day was absolutely ample, and it needed a lot of effort on the part of Karl Schneider to get us additional amounts of food. It wasn't very much but we would have an occasional loaf which he used to steal and he used to get eggs from the farm for us and odd bits of meat like a rabbit. Our garden grew but we had to move the topsoil first so that we could put our clay on the bottom, and then put the top-soil back on top of the clay. It was amazing how much soil we deposited in this way, and it gradually grew and it was raked over nicely and looked smart and attractive. None of the Germans took any notice of this whatsoever. We got some pansy plants in and they were in bloom. This was quite an effort on Karl Schneider's part. He brought in pansies – how the hell he got them in I don't know, but he did – and we put them against the gap between the ground and the edge of the hut so that no one could see underneath what we were doing. Nobody in our camp except for the two huts concerned knew anything about this tunnel. It was even said in a book which was printed, called *Barbed Wire* to raise money for the British Red Cross that this was the only successful tunnel made and the initiative that went into it and the thought, were of extreme brilliance. When you are in a tunnel twelve feet long, the air becomes difficult, particularly when you work with lamps made out of an old margarine ration. The fat that the Germans issued was *ersatz* fat. It used to make an awful lot of carbon so your mouth and nose were absolutely black. This was nearly killing us and we had to stop it. We found an empty hut which the Germans had been using near the entrance to the camp and stripped it of wire. We connected the wire up to ours in the hut by two needles. Then we ran the wire down to our tunnel and so had lights and were able to do another hour's shift at night.

Half-way through the tunnel we ran into an obstacle – there was a great big boulder. Our mathematics were done by some Spaniards, about whom I am going to talk later on; they were Spaniards who had fought in the Spanish Civil War and they were beaten as they were of the Communist faction. They had joined the Palestinian Army and ended up in our camp. By profession two of them were seamen, and one was very good at maths. I used to give them our compass bearings and one used to work out how far we had to go – how many degrees one way, how many degrees the other way and he really kept us on course. We got to this boulder, passed it and got back on our true line. We got right to the edge of the road. On the edge there was a channel to take the surface water. At about this point we were running out of air. As you work down in a tunnel, the stench from a person's body and anything else that might happen to foul the air caused by bad food was so bad that on two occasions I had to make Archie lie on his back so that I could lie back on him to get air because I was nearly suffocated. Means had to be found to get fresh air into this tunnel. We had a collection of Klim tins (milk spelled backwards); these were what the dried milk came in; and we collected these tins from all our neighbours where we could. Then I joined them together and at one end we made a kind of impeller, as in a water pump of a motor car, and we fitted a handle to it which, when turned, would draw air out on one of the circuits and pump air in on the other one. So we had two lines of Klim tins going down, but even that was not sufficient and then we made a pair of large bellows, and what with the three items we managed to get sufficient air to work.

We got about four feet further in and the air was still scarce and I said to Archie, 'Now we will dig straight up and we will get a vent dug,' because, according to the Spaniards' reckoning, we would come out exactly where the gully was on the edge of the road. It would be camouflaged because of the long grass there and we could get a shaft up. So we started working on this upright shaft. Little did I realize what a body-aching job this was to be. To start, I had to lie down, reverse way from the way I had been working, with my face upwards, about two feet six inches above me, and I had no power in my arms to use a tool, so I had to get a knife to cut a circular hole, gradually cutting out the earth so that it was Klim-tin size – about six inches in diameter. It was a very slow, tedious job. All the earth fell in my hair, down my face, in my ears and eyes; and all this strenuous work caused me very bad headaches, and I suffered with neck muscle tiredness. It was truly very fatiguing working in this unnatural way.

After about four days I made it. It was difficult because after you got about an arm's length up from where you were lying, you then had to make a tool to reach through to the top. I pinched a broom handle from the cookhouse –

they were not very pleased about it although they never knew who had it – and on the end I fixed an old bed-lath. This was used as a kind of a knife and I just scratched round and round until I gradually got higher and higher until I managed to get high enough to get a piece of steel tied on to the end of our broomstick and dug like that.

In the end I got to the top after four days of arm- and back-aching toil – and what a relief. This got some fresh air in and I put Klim tins in the best way I possibly could. They went up, I suppose, about four feet. That would be enough to stop any slide of earth, and we stopped work for the night and went to bed and said that was a good day's work, for Archie had been behind.

The next day we worked like hell clearing the accumulated soil, and we crossed the road. It was difficult crossing the road because there was always heavy traffic going over. This tunnel of ours was not strengthened in any way, because we had no timber of any description, as we had stolen everything there was in the camp; we even pinched half a hut which wasn't being used, much to the disgust of the Germans. We pinched it right under their noses and we took the roof off. The Germans raised hell over this but nevertheless we got the roof and we used that for our tunnel but we couldn't get any more, and while we worked under there the tanks and lorries rolled by, but we got right across under the road.

During this time one of our boys had started to get a bit careless with his boots. When he came off the morning shift he used to go on parade without cleaning his boots. I said to him, 'Jock, if you don't clean your boots we are going to have trouble. They will watch our hut.' This was because I had seen Gestapo men walking all around the camp. I had seen them sitting up on a high place watching the various parts of all the camp. Anyway, we crossed the road and we dug a reception area to get away, and we came up within a yard of where we wanted to be. The weather changed suddenly and the rains came, and it came down that road and it rained and rained, the water getting into the gully where our vent was and it flooded the tunnel. We got underneath while it was flooding the tunnel and we stopped the vent up with rags, and we poked sacks and paper and anything else we could find to stop the rain coming in and we did manage to stop the water. Next came the time when we had to bucket out the water that was down there. It wasn't a great amount, but enough, and if we hadn't stopped the vent up it would have been completely flooded. Of course our work became more difficult because of the mud and slime, and we got dirtier, also making our hair like wet dough. Nevertheless we crossed the road and got ready to escape again.

Two days after the tunnel was finished my worst fears were justified. The dirty boots had given us away. There was an upheaval in the camp. Down the road where our hut was came a Gestapo man with a dog and two handlers and this officer walked into our hut and started pushing me about and also my friend, and I took him by his waistcoat and I pushed him out of the hut and I said, 'You are a civilian.'

He started to draw a pistol, and then I said to him in German, 'You draw a pistol on me, you shoot me, then you will get the same, because you will never live to get into this camp again.' He didn't draw a pistol, or shoot at me. By that time the German soldiers had arrived and so we had the military take over.

They arrested us, confined us to our hut and the Camp Commandant came, Col. Aufhammer. He was a very small, sharp-featured man. As a matter of fact, I thought he was a good soldier; he dished our punishment out, and if you were man enough and a good enough soldier you took it. He would give you no more than he was entitled to. I found nothing against him as far as I was concerned. I took my punishment from him. However, he came and sat down on the table – I can see him now, with his little legs swinging – and said, 'Well, my dear Mr. Beeson, you must dig deeper.' With that he arrested me and put me in the bunker and for my troubles I was given twenty-one days' solitary confinement on bread and water. The others got seven days.

My cell measured nine feet by four feet and I had just a

small aperture where light came in. I was woken at six o'clock in the morning and my bed was taken away from me so I had nothing to lie down on. This solitary confinement gives you plenty of time to think and time passes slowly but I did have a couple of cell-mates, spiders. I spent hours watching them. The first thing that I used to look for when I went on 'Solitary' was something to scratch on the wall with, an odd bit of wire or a nail, something to mark the days off with.

Bread and water – one-fifth of a small rye loaf per day, and on the third day a bowl of soup or that's what they called it and that was an extra! I was allowed out for half an hour each day for exercise and I had only a small area to walk around. The PoWs in the main camp used to come near the wire and shout out to me. I remember a Cockney friend of mine shouting out one day, 'Why don't you buy the bloody place, Mole, you must have got sitting tenant rights.'

CHAPTER FIVE

THE TRAIN GAME

WE had been working hard on tunnels for many weeks and we thought it was necessary for us to have a complete change so one of the gang suggested we tried to drive the Germans barmy. And so they had an idea of playing a game of going back home and this is how it started.

About twenty men – Australians, New Zealanders, Englishmen and Scotsmen – got together and said, 'There are eight huts in this row. Let's make them into a train.' In the front part of the row there was a cookhouse – which the Germans had to build for us under the Geneva Convention, so one could heat water and fry something or boil a pudding or make milk, tea or chocolate. We decided that this would be the engine, and the last hut would be the guard's van.

We went to our artistic friends in the camp and asked them to make some posters for us, with the words, 'Back to Blighty' and 'Excursion Trips' and all kinds of advertising matter. Many posters were made – the whitewash and brushes were put into use and all round the camp there were notices such as 'Camp Evacuation'. Many huts had this notice painted on the walls. After about a week, when everything was ready, a notice was put up: 'First Evacuation Train – 9.30 a.m. Monday.' By this time everyone was talking about it. The last notice was plastered up: 'Anyone wishing to catch the Evacuation Train parade at the fire-pond at 09.00 hours.' During this time all the occupants of the eight huts joined in the fun. They made paper dresses, paper hats, and various kinds of uniforms – all from paper. The engine driver, the stoker and the guard all had uniforms and there were also men dressed as porters.

Every morning we had to parade and answer our numbers to ensure that no one had taken French leave. After this parade we started the fun. People came back to their huts and dressed up. The camp knew there was some fun going on and they all wanted to see what it was all about. They had read about the evacuation of the camp. There were other people more interested – the 'snoops'. When the Germans saw what was going on they stood in amazement, not knowing what to make of it all; 9.30 came. The porters were there, carrying bundles of luggage supposed to belong to passengers. There were people arguing and trying to get into a hut, pretending that the railway carriage was full up. More people had arrived than the train could hold. So this started off on a very good footing with the Germans just standing there in amazement. We had about an hour of this to start off with and lots of fun.

The second day the game grew in intensity. They made up a form of taxi which some men had assembled and called the London Taxi Cab Company. There were others who played horses and carts; there were men with bits of string on their arms and behind them were the men who were the coaches and they came into the area which was supposed to be the station. The taxi cab driver got out and pretended to open the door for people to get out. There was an incident in which one particular taxi had brought people with reserved places and when they got to the carriage it was full and so the taxi driver had to get these people to come out by going and fetching the guard and he came followed by the driver and stoker. After a lot of argument out came the people from the carriage and in went the people from the taxi; following them came the horse-drawn coach and in this there were about eight people who also had a reserved place and the same thing happened to them. They didn't mess about; they walked straight into the hut, got the men in the hut and just pulled them out and there was an imitation rough and tumble – nevertheless these men got into the carriage.

By now more Germans had come to watch what was going on and a sergeant of the guard stood there and scratched his head, saying, 'What is all this about! What is all this about!' No one answered him, but they were literally amazed to see all this fun. The driver of one taxi had a mouth-organ and he would use this as a horn and would change up like children do from first to second gear. With his mouth he would make the kind of noises of a missed gear; so he had to change down and then change up again. It was all very hilarious. The driver of the coach and horses had his reins and whip and would say, 'Whooops – steady on now,' and all the words used by good horsemen. The next day came and now I should think about a third of the camp were playing – it was really terrific – there were great crowds of men all around this hut, watching – like a form of variety show. Other members of the camp cottoned on to the game and made up their excursions to join us. There was one group of men from right down the bottom of the camp. They made up a coachload of people going on evacuation and in front of the driver of this coach one person had got a placard 'Evacuation Coach – Full' and they came down the road hooting and honking and singing and shouting. Then more Jerries came in and there was trouble. Into the camp came the *Abwehr* officer, the Camp Commandant and our 'man of confidence', Sgt.-Major MacKenzie. The Camp Commandant came to us and said, 'What is all this going on? What is the matter?' We said that we had no food, no water and the Red Cross parcels had been stopped and we were all going barmy and couldn't control ourselves. We had to do something as we thought we might break out of the camp. We must have our parcels and food. The Germans called in a German doctor. He was a form of psychiatrist and he thought we were all going bonkers. The next day there was a high-ranking German Officer brought in.

Now there was another coachload of passengers – all Londoners with their wonderful Cockney humour. The so-called conductor of this bus was shouting out, 'Up the apples and pears'; then he was naming places like the 'Bone-yard' (Cemetery), the Scrubs (Wormwood Scrubs Prison) and so on. There must have been two thousand men congregated from the fire-pond down at this hut, and many were dressed as women and there were some pretending that they were in a hansom cab and raising their hats and doffing them as they might in Hyde Park on a Sunday morning taking a ride; it was absolutely marvellous to see the amount of excitement that had gone into this and more than anything else how worried the Germans were. They stood there watching the people in the train waving good-bye to the others. They got handkerchieves out and were really having a go.

The Germans were very worried indeed. They fetched Major Brook-Moore, our camp doctor, from the hospital. He said to the high-ranking officer, 'Can you wonder at it? These men have been prisoners for a long time. Their food is insufficient for them to live on; their Red Cross parcels are now becoming short because a lot of Red Cross trains have been smashed. A Red Cross boat has been sunk and as the food you offer them is so terrible, you can expect no more from them. You must do something about it.'

The next day the same thing started all over again – but it had grown even more. I can remember seeing a soldier dressed up as a woman with a very small soldier dressed up as a little boy and they playing mother and son and 'she' was dragging him to the railway station and he didn't want to go. There were arguments and clips on the ears and the 'little boy' sat down on the road and became bad-tempered – stamping his feet and squealing and that created a bit more fun watching him and watching his 'mother' getting him up and heaving him on his way to the station. There were about half-a-dozen men dressed as boys and they had a hoop and a stick. Then the train would leave, the guard blowing his whistle and everyone else imitating the engine, going puff-puff-puff and waving good-bye, crying, screaming and trying to get on to the train. That was how these trains 'left' 383.

We had complained to the high-ranking officer that our sports field was not big enough to exercise the whole camp and that we needed a larger one. We also wanted the ban on people going out to collect wood lifted.

According to the Geneva Convention the Germans were supposed to feed us on the same rations as their own troops but this was not so. Never once in four and a half years did I see a knife and fork meal. We had the cooks' 'Sweet Mystery Soup'; some brands of this liquid included Sauerkraut which was highly laxative; a vile vinegar Celluloid Soup, named for its flavour but made from dried vegetables, since genuine celluloid was scarce; Mock Mangel-Wurzel, squared fibrous chunks of cattle food, fortunately tasteless; Fish Soup, made from the tails and heads of stinking fish, and Caterpillar Soup, in which something was mixed with worms. These delicacies were general in nearly every PoW camp.

Once we got a fish, fruit and nut soup which apparently came from the Turkish Red Cross. They had sent some bulk raisins, nuts and preserves for distribution among the prisoners. What the Huns couldn't eat themselves (they used to help themselves to our parcels) was just tipped into our soup along with the decayed fish. What with the fishbones, raisin pips, prune stones and nut shells to contend with it was a pretty exotic dish. Most of the time our soup was made by British cooks, but the soups that I have spoken about were the specialities of Germans who used to come in and show our cooks how to get rid of their refuse. The first two years of the war were the worst; the Germans had gained everything they set out to. They had no respect for human life whatsoever; the first PoWs had a very bad time all round.

The train game went on for about a week; then Major Brook-Moore came to us and said that he thought there had been enough of it as it was beginning to get out of hand and repercussions were in the offing. So we stopped it, but I am sure that it did a lot of good for we got an additional large area added to our sports field and we were allowed to go out in parties to collect wood again for a while.

I had tried to get back to England by tunnelling, by cutting wire, and had proved that it was impossible to get out by these means. It needed more than strength and brains – you wanted one thing which was not in your power to obtain and that was a lot of luck and without that you just went nowhere. You must have luck on your side.

CHAPTER SIX

I ESCAPE AS A GERMAN NCO

My command of the German language had grown and I was told that I spoke German with a Berlin accent. I could even write German in the old-fashion German handwriting. So I decided to look round for other means of getting out of the camp. One day the idea came to me, 'Why not try and escape as a German officer or German sergeant-major?' I decided to escape as a sergeant-major. A lot of detail and planning had to go into this and so I set about observing German habits – manner of walk, type of uniform, type of war decorations, type of holster and everything about them. Most of all, how was I to make a uniform the same as that of a German? It so happened that the Australian tunic jacket was very similar to the German one, but what I had to do was to cut part of the Australian jacket away in front; it had a double seam going from the collar right down to the bottom of the tunic and I think this was put there to save the wear of the buttons. By undoing this and turning it back into the inside of the tunic it would represent ideally the appearance of a German jacket. Now the next thing was where to get a jacket. My friend, Stropper McDonald, an Australian (he was my 'mucker' which means he was the one who I used to share my Red Cross parcel with), said I could have his. I got my jacket and I went to work with a razor blade and cut the seam of the front part open and reversed it, giving the appearance of that of a German. Epaulettes had to be made and on to this I had to put my rank. There was also beading or silver braid all round the collar and epaulettes and this had to be attached. There were the decorations – I had to know what kind there were, whether I had been in Poland or Africa or on the Russian front. I sat for days and days making epaulettes and reversing this piece of material in the jacket. A lot of needlework was necessary.

I made the epaulettes and then sewed silver paper, that used to come in the BDV* cigarettes on the edges of the epaulettes and all round the collar and it really did look exactly right – not too bright and not too dull. My medal and campaign ribbons were made by an artist from our theatre group and I stitched them on. I tried the jacket on and looked at myself in my odd bit of glass that I used as a shaving mirror and it looked very good indeed. The main difficulty with this job was that I had to be so careful that the German security guards didn't come into the hut while I was making things.

The thing I needed most of all was dye because the Australian jacket was khaki and the German one grey-green. Here Karl Schneider had to do his part and it took rather a long time as he had to get in touch with his people at home near Strasbourg because he could not find any dye of the colour we required in the area of the camp. He got about ten

* Best Divine Virginia.

dyes – the big problem about dyeing khaki uniforms is that there is arsenic in the khaki dye and this upsets the dyeing process. To dye a pair of khaki trousers and a khaki jacket you need a very large receptacle; you also have to boil the dye and to do this under the eyes of the Germans was some activity. It meant that you had to get a drum big enough to hold the jacket and get wood and light a fire under it and boil it; against this was the problem that you had the 'snoops' walking in and out of the huts the whole time. What I had to do was to get this done away from my hut at a hut where there had been no form of activity in the way of escaping or misbehaviour and I got the Spaniard to do this for me. The Spaniard was busy making what I called his 'broth' when a German came along and asked what he was doing and the Spaniard said he was dyeing a dress for the theatre party and by luck (and I needed some by this time) the German guard said 'All right', and took no notice of him. Having dyed the uniform, we had to hang it out to dry somewhere. It was a longish procedure to dry these heavy clothes. So the first thing I did was to take them to a communal lavatory late at night. I fixed up a line and I let the worst of the water drip. While it was dripping out, I sat there on that lavatory I should think for about six hours, and as it dripped I squeezed the garments. Then I had another problem – I was getting this dye on my hands and the dye got under my nails and I was getting in a pretty messy state.

I got most of the water out and the next thing was to dry it thoroughly so that I could crease the trousers and make myself look respectable. I had another near escape with that. I was two huts away from my own and I had taken three other mates with me and one of our blankets and we took up a position so that we could see the Germans coming. We laid the Australian tunic and trousers on the ground and the warmth of the sun helped to get them dry. One day a German 'snoop' was about to walk past us and one of my friends saw him just in time and he pulled the blanket down over the top of the dyed clothes and we played cards with my dyed clothes under the blanket.

The trousers had to be ironed and pressed. I got an old Klim tin, and I made it into a shape of an iron. I got some clay and put it out in the sun in the iron. It got pretty hot in Bavaria, and the clay dried and when it was dry enough I put another piece of metal over the top of it, fixed it together with a pair of pliers and then made a wooden handle and attached it to the iron with bits of other metal so that it looked something like an iron. We put this iron on the stove just near where the chimney comes out and we got it reasonably hot – hot enough anyway for me to put a crease into my trousers. Now I had got my German tunic. The next thing was to get a German hat. That wasn't difficult at all – all I needed was the help of my friend Karl Schneider because he just stole one. Karl was very good for he never asked for anything but I did give him an odd tablet of soap, some coffee and chocolate to send home to his people.

I needed some container to carry escape food in. It was quite simple to make a workman's bag into which I could put chocolate, soap, rye bread and things to barter with. It was made out of the lining of a greatcoat, and it served its purpose very well, but that was not quite enough. I needed something I could pack some chocolate in so that it wouldn't get contaminated by the soap. So I had an idea. One of the Germans, a Sgt.-Major who used to come into our camp, had a holster which was the largest I had seen a German carrying. This holster was just the carrier I required. I borrowed a ruler from the school and walked alongside him talking about the war and other things, and as I walked along I actually took the measurements of his holster. I measured it across and the whole way down. Once he saw me with this rule and asked what I was doing and I said I was just playing about and I continued to talk and managed to get the measurements.

The next problem was how to make it. I got a Red Cross box and I damped it and made it pliable so that I could shape it. With string from the Red Cross parcel which I thinned out I made a thick thread the same as that with which the real holster was stitched – you could see the stitching all the way down – about eight to ten stitches to the inch or something like that. I stitched this exactly like the harnessmaker would do when I saw him repairing the harness for horses, when I was a boy. I made a wonderful job of this holster and into it I packed many bars of chocolate.

One other thing that I needed, the most important of all, was a German *Ausweis* – that is a German identity card. It was not possible to get a full identity card, but I could, by being a bit of a rogue, get an identity card that would allow me, as a German civilian, to travel in the area of Regensburg and Parsburg, for these were carried by German civilians and shown at the gate of our camp to the German guards on duty. The thing was how to get one of these. We had a camera in the camp and the man who operated it was a friend of mine. All I had to do was to steal a German's wallet, take his *Ausweis* out of his wallet and give it to my friend for him to photograph and then give it back to the German without his knowing. It sounds rather a large undertaking but actually when you are in a desperate situation it is amazing what you will think of. This is how it was done.

Along with a couple of my friends I went to the fire-pond which was still being made. The Germans had their coats off so I picked a jacket up and walked slowly away with it until they saw that I had got it and started shouting. As I ran to my hut I gave the wallet to my friend to photograph. He went into his hut and, with all the apparatus ready, took a flash-light photograph of both sides of the *Ausweis*. I ran back and as I ran he gave me the wallet. Followed now by Germans and German soldiers, I pushed the wallet back inside the jacket, threw the jacket at them and ran away in another direction and I was not caught. So the camp then had a negative of a *Dienstausweis*, which is a special kind of identity card to allow one to go in and out of the camp.

Besides this identity card, I had another one which was made for me by a Sgt.-Major of the New Zealand Regiment. This Sgt.-Major was a very special, clever man and he had extraordinary eyes. He printed my *Ausweis* with hairs taken from his head and it was so good that when it was under scrutiny nobody knew it was a false *Ausweis*. It was made from ordinary white cartridge paper with a wash on it. When an exhibition was held in St. James's Palace in London, through the International Red Cross, inmates of prisoner-of-war camps could make things and send them to London, through the Red Cross, to the exhibition. He wrote the Lord's Prayer on the back of a paper the size of a sixpenny piece. The Germans sent him to Munich University to study his marvellous sight.

It was now 22nd August, 1943. It was my intention to escape into the French camp dressed as a German officer and join up with a Frenchman. Then both of us were to travel to Nürnberg, then take the uniform off, having civilian clothes underneath. But my French friend became ill and I was going to go alone.

I needed a date figure marked on my *Ausweis* and my 'forger' was unable to do it for he was also sick. I went to SQMS MacKenzie and asked if he knew anyone who was capable of filling in the quarter date stamp with Roman figures. He said that Sgt. 'Ginger' Suggitt did cartoons, perhaps he would. Suggitt said he would, on condition that he could come with me. Now he had escaped once before, so I agreed. He had to get a uniform made and he asked the theatre costume department, and they made a very good one for him. Then he got all his 'gear' together, and on 28th August, 1943, I went over my plans with him to make sure that we were both aware of the part that each was to play and that we would meet again at 9 p.m., on the twenty-fourth in my hut.

The other men in my hut were astounded by our transformation, for it was a good 'turn out'. As for myself I must admit that I did have some feeling of trepidation, remembering the notices that had been posted around the camp about escapers and here we were dressed as German NCOs. We did not hang about very long in the hut, and the first thing that I did was to create a kind of reliance in myself of the fact that I was now a German. One of the huts opposite mine was showing some light, but it was forbidden to show light; everything had to be 'blacked out'. I went across to the door, banged on it and shouted *'Verdunkel'*, meaning 'Black your lights'. I travelled a few more yards and did the same to another hut and by this time I had gained a lot of confidence in myself.

Ginger and I walked very slowly along the camp's main road and I sometimes spoke to him in German. (He did not speak German, only French.) But by speaking to him as we walked it gave me confidence, and also showed to any German soldier that might be about that we were going off duty. Altogether it was nearly a mile from my hut to the main gates that led out through the camp on to the main road which was to take us to Parsberg and the station.

An Englishman came to me and said, 'Please will you ask these guards to let me out as I need to go back to the hospital.' It so happened that this soldier was a bandsman out of the Durham Light Infantry and he sat next to me in our accordion band and we had played together many hours. I thought that he would recognize me and give the game away, but he did not. By this time I don't think I had one heart but twenty. I was so flabbergasted that it just took the wind out of my sails for a moment and I said to him in German, 'I am not a child's maid to look after men who cannot obey orders and cannot do their duty. Go away! Stay in the camp tonight and come back in the morning because it is dark now and I will not permit the guards to let you out.' He looked hesitant. I then said if he did not go away I would put him in the bunker for the night. He went away.

Then I turned to the German guards and shouted to them, 'Open the gates! Open the gates!' They opened the gates and we passed our first obstacle. Then Suggitt and I were on our way towards the main gate.

Imagine the feeling we had now, having met this obstacle and having the life frightened out of us and with the worst part still to walk. I think we had diminished in size a hundred-fold. However, the part we had to walk now was about two hundred yards and this would bring us to the main gate, but before we got there, on each side of the road there were huts, which on the right-hand side were occupied by German guards not on duty and on the left-hand side was a place where they kept spare ammunition, bread and odd bits of meat, such as it was. There were always Germans going in and out from there. We had to walk past these Germans. That was a frightening experience, but nevertheless one that we coped with very well indeed. I got to the main gate and there were two German guards there – or should have been there, but one was down the road talking to somebody. On the other side of the main road was the whole of the German encampment, German military, etc., and the other guard was talking to the guard in the watch-tower, where the machine-gun was. I had learnt to swear in German and I shouted at them and they came. I said, 'What are you doing down there? You should be at the gate.' They were scrambling about and I kept saying, 'Where are your keys? Get the keys and open this gate and let me get out. I have been in an English camp too long.' They opened the gate and we were outside.

We had been walking for about half an hour when we were challenged by a German sentry. I told the German that he had done well in making us stop for identification. This pleased the guard and we were soon on our way again.

Not long after this we had another frightening experience. In front of us there were lights shining and I could see that they were lights from a vehicle, and I thought that a road block had been set up. As we got closer we could see about six German soldiers and I thought this is the end. We kept walking; no one attempted to stop us and we walked through the Germans. They gave us the German salute and I returned it. It appeared that the soldiers were on a night exercise laying telephone cables. We continued our journey towards Parsberg.

The road was windy and downhill for quite a distance with pinewoods on each side. When we thought that we were about five kilometres from Parsberg we entered the wood. In this wood we removed our German uniforms, dug holes in the ground with sticks and our bare hands and buried our disguise.

We broke off branches from a fir tree to keep the hoar frost off us. We had short spells of sleep and, while we rested, it gave us time to collect our senses. We had about five kilometres to walk to Parsberg station and our train was due to leave at 6.30 a.m. About 5 a.m. we started to prepare our walk to the station. First we had to remove the branches, brush off the hoar frost, clean our clothes, remove bits of twig and moss from our boots. We collected hoar frost and with this we washed our faces and had a 'dry' shave which was not very pleasant early in the morning when your face is so cold, but it was necessary to be clean and tidy so that we did not attract unnecessary attention.

We arrived at Parsberg station about 6.15 a.m. I was about to go to the ticket office when who should I see but the Gestapo officer who had caught me in my own camp, the man who I had pushed out on to the road from my hut and had told him, 'If you shoot me you will never live to get out of this camp alive.' If he had shot me now there would have been no redress whatsoever. I had broken the law. I was in civilian clothes. I was very frightened and it was difficult for me to collect my thoughts. It seemed hours before I could pull myself together but of course it was only seconds. I walked past him and went straight to the place where one got a ticket and I asked for a ticket to Nürnberg, and the girl said, 'You have plenty of time, the train does not arrive yet.' So I had to come away from the ticket office. Can you imagine my feelings now? Here I am, an escaped PoW dressed in civilian clothes, having to speak in a foreign tongue, with an officer who could shoot me at any moment, and not knowing any of the German habits. I went on to the platform and I came back as I could hear a train coming in. I said to this girl, 'The train is coming in?' and she replied, 'No, not yet.' So I walked away thinking that I must be barmy as I could hear a train coming. I went out on to the platform again. There were not many people, not more than

70

twenty, and Suggitt was there. We could now see the train in
the distance and I turned back to go to the office, but the
Gestapo man was there, so I did not bother to get tickets,
but went back on to the platform.

The train came in and we got into it. Now this was a single
line track and we wanted to go to Nürnberg, but unfortunately this train was going to Munich, but we were
forced to take this train to give us shelter from the German
officer. How on earth he never spotted me I cannot understand. He knew me well. How could he have missed me, for
we had looked at each other as we passed?

The ticket inspector came into the compartment and
asked for our tickets and I said we hadn't got them and that
we had not time and had to rush to get into the train. So we
bought a ticket for each of us to go to Regensberg. She also
fined us for travelling without a ticket – a couple of marks
extra. If you travelled without a ticket in those days in Germany, you were fined on the spot. We got out at Regensberg
and had to wait for a train to go to Nürnberg which passed
through our own station of Parsberg. Just after the train
had gone through Parsberg this same ticket collector came
again and she said, 'Tickets,' and I told her we didn't
have any tickets. She then asked why we were travelling
again without any tickets. She said, 'An hour or so ago I
fined you for travelling to Regensberg with no ticket and
now you are travelling through here to Nürnberg with no
ticket again; how do you explain this?' I said, 'That is very
simple, we had to go to Regensberg in the first instance to do
work; we are Belgian Conscripted Labour and we had to go
to meet the Führer of our working party but when we arrived he said we were to return to Nürnberg and report to
the head at the marshalling yard because the British
bombers had caused a lot of damage and it was necessary
for extra staff to go there.' She accepted this explanation and
we bought the tickets and paid the fine again. The journey
was an interesting one – beautiful scenery, and it was
interesting to listen to the conversation of the Germans in
the train. One woman, aged about fifty, had just lost her

husband and her son had been wounded in a recent RAF raid at Nürnberg. He worked, it seemed to me, in the signal-box, and she was going to the hospital to see him. With her she carried a basket of 'windfall' apples – what measly things they were for a sick man. It was not possible for her to pick her own fruit from her own tree as the fruit had to go to the troops in Russia. This elderly woman was speaking to a young woman of about twenty-four or twenty-five years and she was full of sorrow because her husband had been killed on the Russian front, leaving her with two children. They were both very pathetic sights to see.

About five kilometres out from Nürnberg we began to see the results of the excellent bombing by the British. A short way away was the famous sports-platz where one of the early Olympic Games took place – I think 1936 – and on the other side were the remains of the Lager where the Hamburg evacuees were housed and then the mangled wrecks of locomotives and wagons, with all the factories on both sides of the track completely demolished.

Our object at Nürnberg was to try and catch the express train which would take us to Metz. I found that we had four hours to wait. At this time in Germany if anyone was caught loitering he was challenged by the Police and asked for his identity and work papers. So we couldn't wait about anywhere. We took a walk around town and we were thirsty. We came to a place where we saw a sign on the wall which said this was the home of Wagner. Next door there was a guest house. We went inside and we had a mug of lager. And that was very good beer. From here we went into a newsreel cinema and saw the most amazing film. It was the evacuation of the German fleet from Brest. That didn't raise our hopes very much because we saw our torpedo boats being sunk, our aircraft being shot down and photographs showing how clever the Germans really were.

We went back to the railway station and stood in four different queues but not without mistakes and incidents. Whilst in the fourth queue a man wearing a swastika walked straight past the queue up to the office window, pushed his

72

way in and bought a ticket. Another German, apparently a non-party man, stopped him and asked him what right he had to obtain a ticket in such a manner. A fight started and the party man got the worst of it before the fight was stopped by the station police. A blonde girl in front of me turned round and said, 'You see what one gets for wearing the swastika.'

Luckily, I was not forced to answer because the queue had started moving again. When I was about to buy my ticket an old lady rushed up to me and said, 'Please buy me a ticket for Crailsheim. I have no time to stand in the queue. The train goes in five minutes.' I agreed; she gave me a ten mark note and I bought her the ticket. Now I made another mistake. I wanted to go to Heilbronn, north of Stuttgart, and the ticket that was given to me was for Heilbronn, and that was only about twenty kilometres west of Nürnberg. If I had been more careful and checked my change, I should have realized that there was a mistake, but I did not. The place I wanted to get to was a hundred and fifty kilometres further on so naturally I would have had to pay more money than the few marks that I did. Luck was against us again, because just before we got to Heilbronn, the ticket collector came into our compartment and asked for our tickets and I showed him them and he said 'next stop'; so we had to get out. From here we walked along the path near the railway to a station called Winklesgreuth. During this walk of about twenty kilometres, we had to hide from a party of Hitler Jugend who were out on exercise with their Führer, a boy of about fourteen. They were terrible little devils. They had the right to demand identification papers. We waited until it was clear and then we continued our walk. Later we were stopped by a railway worker and I put him off by asking for a drink of water as he was standing near his house which belonged to the German railway, and he gave me a drink and a couple of plums. After this I took two more and that didn't please him very much and we left him cursing me.

We arrived at the station of Winklesgreuth. It was a small

station, and there was a girl there who was station-master-cum-everything and I bought two tickets for Stuttgart.

Before the girl would give me these tickets, she told me, as I was a foreign worker, I had to fill in a form so that they knew my whereabouts. I duly filled in this form, giving lots of false information, of course. The girl looked at it and there were no queries whatsoever. I even pulled out my identity card, which was of no use whatsoever, but I just took it out and pretended I was looking at the number of my pass, and she accepted all this very well.

Now we were on the train going from Winklesgreuth to Stuttgart, but when we arrived at Dombühl, the train had to stop and everybody had to get out and through the loud speaker system it was announced, 'The train to Stuttgart . . .' and then I couldn't understand what it said as the dialect was so bad. If you stand on London stations and listen to the loud speakers it is difficult to understand in our own country, let alone a German dialect coming through a speaker. There must have been a lot of trouble somewhere because there were lots of police on the station and it was all chaotic. There was a train in the station and I said to Suggitt, 'Come on, let's get in this one.' The train instead of going north went south. It was only a small train and it went to a place called Nördlingen. So we went to Nördlingen and that was the end of the journey for it, and so we had to get out. Once again we were asked for our tickets and we showed our tickets going to Stuttgart, but we were at Nördlingen and the girl took us to the Station Master. He was a very officious man, and very important in his own eyes.

He took us into his office and laid the law down to us and he fined us double the amount that we should have paid. We also had to pay for the ticket from Dumbühl to Nördlingen and from Nördlingen back to Dombühl. However, we got out of this difficulty and on the way back a strange thing happened. I was going between two carriages where they join together and as I was passing over these steps I bumped into a man and he pushed his hands into me and he gave me the 'thumbs-up' sign. I like to think he was another Englishman escaping. I never did find out.

We got back to Dombühl and apparently whatever the trouble was was all over. We got on to the train and started our journey towards Stuttgart. One of the difficulties of travelling by *Schnellzug* (express train) was that there was more control. There was the Gestapo to control it and the station or railway police who also controlled it. They asked for tickets; they searched for German soldiers taking 'French leave'; they searched for foreigners like us 'Belgian workers' who were without papers; they searched for everything. It was not my intention to travel by a fast train; it was my intention to always travel by the small trains as there was less control and catching this fast train was our undoing. I said to Suggitt, 'You go up the front end of this carriage and I will go the other end.' We hadn't been away from one another for more than half an hour when the Gestapo caught Suggitt. They must have had some difficulty in finding me because the train was absolutely packed – people standing everywhere. I had managed to get myself right up near the lavatory door, among the soldiers who were lying on the floor. However, a Gestapo officer turned everyone over and found me. He took us to a compartment and made four people get out and he gave us a seat and sat down himself and one of his underlings sat down also. We had to admit that we were Englishmen and that we were escaping. I showed him our Stalag discs. He opened the flap of his revolver holster and said, 'If you try to escape we shall shoot you – if you behave yourselves you will be taken to our headquarters and then sent back to your camp. You will get your punishment at your camp.' So the game was up.

They searched me. 'Chocolate,' they said, with surprise. And then they found about five hundred cigarettes which surprised them even more. What a song and dance they made about this. No wonder, because at this time Germans were rationed to three cigarettes per day and no chocolate. What should I do with the chocolate and cigarettes? So I asked to go to the lavatory and the underling came with me and by doing this I had to pass along the corridor and by this time everyone knew I was an *'Englander'* and I thought I would give them some propaganda and so as I walked along

75

I put my hands in my pockets and gave most of my chocolate and many cigarettes away without the police knowing. It was a good chance, I thought, to let people know that England was not as short of food as the Germans published. On my way back two persons squeezed my hand in appreciation and one said 'Long live England'. I had quite a conversation with the Gestapo men and also with two girl ticket collectors. One asked for a piece of chocolate and I was about to give it when the Gestapo officer stopped me. The girl said that no one would know if she ate it but the officer said it was against the Führer's orders. But I did give her some when they were not looking.

I was taken to the main police station called Geheimnisstadt Bureau at Stuttgart, taken to an examination chamber and stripped. The warders or whatever they were called looked in my mouth, in my ears, in between my toes, switched on the arc lights, made me bend down with my back to them. Then they searched my clothes and found only a few cigarettes and some chocolate and a bar of soap, which they retained until I was released to the military authorities. I was taken downstairs to, I suppose, the officer in charge of the police station. I am not sure, but he was a very high-ranking man and he was immaculately dressed. He had black breeches with terrific flares and his tunic was green with a black velvet collar. There was a lot of gold on the collar. The boots were the same kind as one wears in the hunting field only they fitted much more tightly and were of a lighter material, possibly kid. The buttons on his tunic were made of real bone and I found out afterwards that they were made from antler of deer. He asked me lots of questions and I told him that as a prisoner-of-war, Stalag Number 2225, I was not obliged to answer any questions except that I was a British soldier and that I was a Staff Sergeant. My army number was 7612882. And that was all I was obliged to tell him under the Geneva Convention. They got a bit naughty and slapped me across the face and he said, 'You will answer my questions.' I said, 'I have answered your questions, sir.' I then said, 'I have given you my rank and

76

name and my army number and also my Stalag number and that I have escaped from a prisoner-of-war camp called Hohenfels not far from Parsberg.' 'Are you going to answer these questions?' he said. 'Where did you get your information from? Where were you going to?' etc. etc. I said, 'Sir, I am travelling on speculation – I am trying to find out where I am going as I go along.' So he gave me another wallop. He then called in a dog handler, who came in and stood two Alsatian dogs in front of me. He said, 'Put your hands on your head – both hands.' This I did. He then said, 'I promise you, if you take your hands off your head the dogs will have you.' I suppose he must have thought I didn't believe him. He walked to the end of the room and so did the handlers and he then suggested that I took my hands away. I did and, my goodness, those dogs would have had me, so my hands went very quickly back on my head again. He said, 'Now I am going to lunch. I shall be away at least two hours. When I come back I want the answers.' He was away for more than two hours and they were the longest two hours I have ever spent in my life. I tried to move my arms, but these dogs were terrible. If I tried to relax my elbows there was the lifting of the lips and when I saw those teeth and fangs showing I thought, I don't mind being shot if it has to be death but not pulled to pieces by these things. So I had to keep my hands on my head for over two hours.

The officer returned and said, 'Well, are you going to answer my questions.' I said, 'I have already, sir, as I told you.' He then called in two officers. They made me march up an iron staircase. We walked to the very top, along a corridor and I was on the top floor of the main prison of Stuttgart. He put me into a cell – a cell for two. There were ten of us. There were three Frenchmen, two Hungarians, two Rumanians, an Austrian and a German. The conditions were terrible, the air was foul and there was no ventilation. I never thought it was possible for so many bugs to be in such a small place. I stripped off when I got in this cell as the others had done because I didn't want bugs and lice in my clothes again and also it was hot. I hung my clothes on an old pipe which I suppose was the chimney pipe of the stove. There were so many of us in this cell that it was impossible to lie down – we used to have to stand and rest against one another. The next morning I was bitten so badly that I could hardly see out of my left eye. And only slightly with my right as I had had a good hiding and my right eye was practically closed. Midday came and the warder arrived with food. He saw me asleep and came and clipped me as it was forbidden to rest during the day and one had to stand to attention when the cell door was opened.

In the afternoon I was taken before the chief for interrogation again. He asked me the same questions and he had the dogs also. He wanted to know where I was going, how did I get the German marks (I had about 1,000 marks on me then), how did I manage to get such an amount of German currency. I still didn't tell him. He wasn't happy at all and I got a couple more good wallops. I was sent back to my cell and that night I did not sleep again. I had just dozed off with my knees under my chin in a sitting position, when the air-raid siren sounded. We soon heard in the distance the drone of engines, and the sound of the German anti-aircraft guns. It got nearer and at one time the building was simply swaying because there were some large guns not far from us and every time they fired at our aircraft it shook the building. The RAF must have dropped some fair sized 'eggs' because in the cracks of our small fanlight, which was only about eighteen inches square, being our only means of ventilation, we could see great flames coming up from the town and it was very heartening to hear our aircraft giving the Germans such a pasting. It was also very frightening for us because if a bomb had hit our prison that would have been our lot, as there was no means of escape.

We only had one meal a day, at midday and that was a form of soup – terrible stuff. At six o'clock in the morning we were awakened by two guards and outside there was a trolley and a large container of coffee, and into a bucket was put sufficient for each of us to have a mug-full. While we were drinking this one man had to go with the other guard to get a bucket of water and cloth and wipe up all the urine and excreta from the floor of the cell, because no one was allowed out at night and in all we were only allowed out twice a day to relieve ourselves in whatever shape or form it was necessary. This place just stank. It got inside our stomachs and every part of us, the pores of our skin, our hair. Every time I breathed I felt like being sick. I was in this cell altogether about nine days. In the middle of the night the door was opened and an Austrian soldier was thrown in; he was drunk. The lights were switched on and I would have never thought it possible to see so many bugs; the wall was covered with them. They were so thick that if you had painted the wall with glue or treacle and then taken a handful of raisins and thrown them on to the wall that was how thick the bugs were. All our bodies were bitten by these things. There wasn't a part of our bodies that wasn't being attacked. The inhabitants of this cell were prisoners, Germans who had been caught in black market trading, deserters and farm workers who had tried to escape. Most of these, both men and women (there were many women in this prison), were sent to the Todt organization for work on the Russian front. A German soldier who was in this cell explained to me that he had been on the Russian front and that he had got frostbite in his feet and had lost several toes. He was dismissed from the army and sent out into civvy street to work. He was unable to work very well and was often away sick. The authorities were not satisfied with his conduct and his efforts and they sent him to prison.

On my ninth day I was taken to a special escapee camp at Ludwigsburg where I remained for about nine days prior to going back to my own camp at Hohenfels. While at Ludwigsburg I met all nationalities – Serbs, Dutch, Russian, French, Belgians. One day a Dutchman asked if I would help with a concert because it was Queen Wilhelmina's birthday. We were living just like cattle. Nevertheless we got a concert going and every National Anthem was sung and they asked me to sing two other patriotic pieces. So I sang Land of Hope and Glory, and England My Island Home. The Germans did not approve of this concert because they said it had not been organized or sanctioned by them, so it had to end, but not before we had our fun, with the result that the Jerries fired a few rounds to help us close the concert. Soon after I was taken back to 383.

CHAPTER SEVEN

BACK TO 383

WHEN the German guard arrived at Ludwigsburg to escort me back to Hohenfels, the officer in charge gave my escort strict instructions that if I made any attempt to escape I was to be immediately shot. The officer had a head so big and in my opinion so empty to make a remark like this; for how could I escape in my present condition? It had been twenty-one days since I escaped from Stalag 383 with little food except the rubbish that the Germans gave me in my cell. I had lost just over twenty-eight pounds for I weighed eleven stone in 383 and now I was under nine stone. My general condition was very bad, all my German money and escaping 'gear' had been confiscated, and I was very weak because I had been 'roughed up'. To be honest I was looking forward to going back, because nothing could have been much worse than Stuttgart.

The journey back was uneventful, leaving Ludwigsburg early morning and arriving at Parsberg station about 5 p.m. From here I had to march about fifteen miles to 383 and by the time I got there I was just about all in, and so was the German guard.

On my arrival Hauptmann Blumm greeted me and asked me how I got out. I refused to say, so he said to the chief interpreter, 'Bring Beeson's friend in.' This made me wonder what was going on, because I had no friend connected with this escape. My friend was brought in. It was a dummy with its face made from a flannel and dressed in a British greatcoat. He sat it down in the chair and I burst out laughing. The German officer, second in command, gave me such a back-hander he knocked me straight across the floor. This dummy had been placed in my bed in my hut just after I left the camp. When the Germans came in to check the number of people in that hut, as I was on control, meaning that I had to report three times a day, they saw the dummy asleep in the bed and didn't bother to check or wake him. When they took this dummy to the Commandant to see if they could gain any information from him – he no speak! Blumm interrogated me; he asked me how I got out – where I had been – how I travelled – how I had been caught. He asked me all about my escape and I replied the same to him as I had on previous occasions and it was the same as I had always said when I had been captured. I mentioned that the Geneva Convention said that all I was required to do was to give my name, rank and number. He asked me over and over again; he tried to wriggle out of me where I got the money from and how I got my civilian clothes. He tried everything. He promised to send me to Torgau, a notorious concentration camp. Then his second-in-command started to question me. He said, 'I suppose Beeson, it was you who organized the escape over the wire.' I said, 'I know nothing of the escape over the wire.' So he said, 'You must have done because that was how you got out.' So I asked, 'Did I?' I continued, 'If that was the way I got out, that will suit me. You know now.' He said, 'Was it the way you got out?' So I replied, 'I am not going to answer that question.' He then slapped me across the mouth and really split my lip, and I had a really bad cut. From that day to this I am sure they were never certain how I got out. I really think they thought that I got over the wire.

It pleased Hauptmann Blumm that I was back, no doubt about that, because nobody had ever escaped successfully from this camp, so I got twenty-eight days' solitary confinement. During this stay, the man in the next cell and myself planned an escape. I suppose it was a foolhardy scheme but we had to keep the Germans at it and keep ourselves fit. In all, this 'bunker' would hold twenty men, who were put into cells which were eleven feet by four feet, about ten feet high. For my bed I had a table with a few boards on it and every other day I was allowed a paliasse. I always had two blankets. There was no window in this cell except a very small light which was about ten inches by five. That was the only light and the only air that came in. In the middle of the door there was a spy-hole and it was convex so that the Germans could stand outside and look in and see what I was doing without coming into the cell.

I was awakened at 6 a.m. and I had a mug of water or coffee. I was allowed to go to the toilet and wash myself and while I was there the guard stood watch over me. Then I returned to my cell. I was not allowed to lie on my so-called bed during the day and by the time six o'clock at night came I was pretty tired. At midday I had my daily ration, being one-fifth of a loaf and another cup of coffee, and this was to last me all day. Every third day I had a supplement of a bowl of German soup. You could either call it celluloid soup or what the hell you like, but it was awful. For twenty-eight days this is where I rested my weary bones and I could feel them all.

Next door to me there was a Pole named Baronowski. He had escaped and it was reputed that he had killed a German and he was in this bunker awaiting trial and undoubtedly he was going to be shot if proved guilty. The Germans did not have much time for the Poles and it was very evident that he was going to get his final 'passing out card'. He told me one day when we were in the toilet that the boards in the place where I went to relieve myself were cut. All one had to do was to remove the excreta bucket and lying on the ground was a big pair of pliers. It was dark behind the hut and quite easy to cut the surrounding wire. He had planned to go out that way and he wanted me to go with him and so I said I would think about it. However, I didn't go out with him because the next day he was taken away and I don't know what happened to him.

Once during my stay in this bunker Col. Aufhammer made a visit and he brought with him some high-ranking officer – a General I think he was. The General said to me, 'You are here once more, Herr Beeson,' and I said, 'Yes, I am here, unfortunately, once more.' So he said to me. 'Now you know that the Germans are too clever for you and that it is not possible for you to escape.'

I said, 'On the contrary, sir, when one goes through life you learn by your mistakes, and he is a poor man that doesn't learn by his mistakes, and I have learned a lot.' He then asked what I meant. I said, 'It means exactly this, sir, that I shall try and escape again. I want to get back home.' He then became sarcastic and said, 'May I have the pleasure of asking you when you will go out.' I said, 'Yes, you may, sir. I shall be out on the 1st of May, or thereabouts.' He stamped his foot on the ground and said, 'Oh, my God.' He then said to the Colonel, 'We will leave him. This man is mad.' And that was the last I ever saw of the German General, for on the 1st of May, 1944, I made my final escape.

I arrived back in the main camp at the end of October, 1943. I went to my hut, No. 201. All my pals were there to meet me. In this hut were nine of the hardened escapers. In all there were twenty-two or twenty-three hardened escapers and we had to live in three huts next door to one another and we were controlled morning, midday and last thing at night. My friends had made a special dinner for me; they had saved all my Red Cross parcels, so I had quite a feast. Of course they all wanted to know all about my journey, the mistakes I made, and to have information about railways and controls and everything escapers wanted to know.

Our 'Man of Confidence' came to see me and said, 'My goodness it looks as though you have had a rough time. I will send for Major Brook-Moore.' A 'Man of Confidence', or 'Vertraute' officer, was voted by the whole camp to deal with any problems that they may have, whether they be domestic, or acts contrary to the Geneva Convention. This man has the right to see the Camp Commandant and International Control Officers as for example Swedish and Swiss

Red Cross when they visited the camp. It was a difficult job. The first eighteen months of the war the Germans did not recognize the Geneva Convention; it was only after the British had taken German PoWs they started to do so.

He said to me, 'You look like a bloody ghost, Beeson,' and I said, 'I feel like it.' 'Well,' he said, 'I will make arrangements for you to have special hospital Red Cross parcels in addition to your own.' Make no mistake, I had had a very rough time, and I was ill.

But before he could do this he had to get permission from the Camp Commandant and he would not hear of it. His contention was that I, being the most notorious prisoner in the camp, had asked for my difficulties and the condition that I found myself in. There was only myself to blame. However, I did get my parcels, thanks to Brookie.

While I was away on my last excursion the Germans had posted in the camp notices that an area which extended to a twenty-mile radius was known as a 'defence area' – closed to all personnel without permit. Now that was a bit of a teaser because I told the German I was going to go out of camp on or about 1st May and I intended to do this; but how, at the moment, I did not know. The first thing for me to do was to get myself well and fit again. I had a great friend in my time of being ill. I was mentally sick too. 'Stropper' McDonald, my 'mucker', was a damn good friend to me and he helped me mentally. I needed someone like that and he encouraged me to build myself up as quickly as possible and 'then have another go at the bastards', as he put it.

Escaping was a serious and dangerous sport and could cost you your life; it was no idle German threat to murder an escaper. This was emphasized by posters and handbills distributed throughout the camp. Our camp was in the centre of a very large military area and one read such notices as 'Stay in your Stalag where you will be safe' or 'You will certainly lose your life if you escape'. These notices were printed in bold red and were posted on many buildings in our camp.

The Chief Security Officer promised more than once to

send me to a concentration camp where, he said, I would get the 'full treatment'. Of course I was a thorn in their sides as I had spent one-fifth of my prisoner-of-war life in solitary confinement.

The threat of murdering us was not to be taken lightly, for they had committed some murderous acts. We knew all about the butchery of fifty Royal Air Force officers from Camp Luft 3 in Bavaria, and there was no reason to suppose that these posters were printed as bluff.

I certainly was instrumental in getting twelve French soldiers back to France because I heard from them through prisoner-of-war letters received in the French camp. In all there were about a hundred and fifty men who got out of this camp through my organizing the means to cross the Rhine. This kind of escape was only suitable to French-born prisoners-of-war, because the German scrutiny and control on the French side was intense and it was so easy to stop a bullet. I only tried to get two Englishmen away by this means and they were both recaptured in the French camp.

This escape I called the Rhinneck Crossing, because the rivers Rhine and Neckar had to be crossed. Two Frenchmen only and myself knew the details of this evacuation. We knew a Frenchman who had married a German girl prior to the war and lived at Regensburg on the Danube. He spoke both German and French fluently. He was a lorry driver and journeyed to Paris and to other large French towns. He knew men and women associated with the French Resistance and was able to get French identity cards and work permit cards. He took frightful risks because the escaper had to have many qualities and I am sorry to say that many men I helped to get away from the French camp did not have all the qualities that were required when facing unusual and difficult situations. No person ever leaked any information but I am sure that Hauptmann Blumm knew that I played a fair part in it.

I tried to get Ted Hartman and myself away by this means but somebody 'shopped' me and the German Security soldiers picked me up on a 'snap parade' in the French camp. It was from this recapture that Hauptmann Blumm took me to the Commandant's Office and promised that if I did not give him all the information that he required he would send me to a concentration camp, where they would get the information, and he said I would be fortunate to get out alive, but he got no information although I had a 'bit of a going over' – with a few lumps and bumps.

Hauptmann Blumm asked me how many cameras were there in the camp. I replied that no one had told me that he owned a camera. I knew what he was looking for; he was trying to find the photo of a PoW who had been shot while under the trip-wire picking dandelion leaves. He had raided the camp a few times to find this photo. Once he sent in 200 soldiers to search for the camera but he never found it. Then he asked me if I was the one who organized the attempted escape of a PoW hidden under a stack of coal which was being unloaded in the German quarters and I told him I was an engineer not a miner and I got a wallop for that reply.

After this Blumm made us have our photos taken once a month, that was twenty-two of us who had escaped at some time.

When Blumm had finished with me I got another twenty-one days' solitary.

Every day into 383 came the *Abwehr* officers, special guards, and their particular job was to search huts for tunnels, anything that could help a prisoner escape, goods of various kinds that had been brought into the camp and exchanged for what we had to offer, such as soap, cigarettes, coffee. These guards were known as 'snoops' and the corporal in charge was known as 'Hamburg Harry'.

If you wanted anything, Harry would get it – at a price. He spoke English perfectly, having lived in America for twenty years, and he was a calm, collected man, far removed from the other Germans I knew. He never tried to get too friendly with us, which kept him in good grace with his master, but he was an inveterate racketeer and brought many forbidden articles into the camp. I never dealt with him because I did not trust him, but many did and he took thousands of cigarettes out of the camp. (These were sent to us by relatives.) To me he was a typical Nazi. He did all this black market – on a big scale. Other Germans who did business on a minute scale were caught and severely punished, so I suspected that he was planted there. His proper job was in the Camp Post Office, where he would check the parcels from England and he knew near enough what came in. His main distribution centre was Munich and from there the bulk of the forbidden articles came into our camp.

One of the articles he smuggled in was a Leica camera. It was for one of my friends. I forget how many cigarettes he had to give for it; I know it was several thousand but it was a very useful piece of equipment to have. Hamburg Harry made a big profit out of this and he 'conned' my friend. To get even with him and to put us on a more than equal footing, we arranged that we should take a photograph of him doing black market with us. We told him that we wanted a whole German sausage. He brought it to our hut and two of us took him between our two huts and started dealing. I got to arguing with him and, while this was going on, my friend surreptitiously took a photograph of him handing over this large sausage. Now this was gilt-edged security for us, for we could turn the tables on him if we ever needed.

One day a fellow PoW came to me and said, 'Is your nickname "Mole"?' I said that it was, and he said that Hamburg Harry had caught him with his radio and there were then only two radios in the camp. Could I help? We found the 'snoop' and he still had the radio. I said, 'Would you come with me to my hut as I have something of great interest to show you,' and he said, 'What is it?' But I said that he must come with me and see it with his own eyes.

I had aroused his curiosity and I think he thought that I was about to make a deal with him. So I was, but not what he had in mind. When I got to the hut I said to him, 'How much for the radio,' and he said, '5,000 cigarettes.' I replied, 'I am not going to give you one smoke. I will exchange this photo for the radio; if not I will give it to your Captain on parade tomorrow morning.' We did our deal and I said to my friend in front of Harry, 'You do not talk of this incident,' and that closed the deal.

The French PoW camp was only about a mile from ours and it was from this camp that I organized the escape of thirty-nine Frenchmen. It was easy for me to get into the camp because French PoWs had to come and work in ours or bring in food rations and the Red Cross and personal parcels from home. All I had to do when the guards were not looking was to change overcoats and caps with a Frenchman. This camp was not so difficult to get out of as ours. I found a suitable place to cut the wire. This was near a disused stable. Although it was padlocked, a sharp blow from a hammer would spring the levers and it would come open; it meant that someone not escaping could put it back and make it look as if it was still locked.

Two Frenchmen knew a French lorry driver who drove a lorry from Regensburg to Paris, and one of these men gave me the address of his grandmother in Paris, should I ever need it. I did at a later date. The escape took place and about ten were never recaptured. To my knowledge the Germans never did find out how they got out; but, my goodness, it did worry them, and they tightened their security in our camp. In all I went into this camp three times, using the same method on each occasion.

The second time I went in, I took Ted Hartman, of the Black Watch, with me; he was a tough, sensible man and knew a lot about unarmed combat. I thought that he would be a good man to travel with; he was very strong and had lots of stamina. We got into the French camp by the same means, and we were to go out on a working party the next day, get to a rendezvous near Regensburg and go by lorry to Paris.

We arrived in the French camp about 11 a.m. It had just started to snow and by 2 p.m. there were about two inches of snow; by dusk there were about four inches, and in the morning it was over a foot deep. This meant that no working party could go out, so if we got away from the working party the next day, we would have to make up a day which we had lost so as to get to our meeting-place on time. But this was not to be, because it snowed for a week, and when it snows in Bavaria it really snows.

Now we really had a problem. In the British camp were the two Frenchmen who had changed places with us. Somehow we had to get back and quickly, but the problem was how. However, it was soon resolved. We saw twenty German soldiers advance into the camp. A parade was called and every French soldier, including the cooks, were made to go on parade. The guards searched all the buildings, got everyone out and the officer posted sentries all along our ranks – four in each rank. Then the officer in charge with some of his special 'snoops' made the first four march three paces forward, looked at them and then the next and the next and next, and they looked at every man. By this time it was obvious that they were looking for me. I knew that my chances of not being observed were very slim. I was in the middle of the column wearing a French greatcoat and a balaclava, and I said to a Frenchman standing next to me, 'Lend me your glasses,' which he did. These were coloured glasses because of the snow.

The ranks were moved forward and checked, and this went on until it came to my rank, and by this time my heart was well and truly in my mouth. I moved forward on command; they looked at me and passed me and I thought luck was with me, when all of a sudden Hauptmann Blumm spotted me, took my glasses off, made two guards arrest me and march me to the Kommandantur.

Here I had a tough gruelling. He wanted to know who else was with me, and promised that unless I told him, he would send me to a concentration camp. He spoke to me in English and I said that his dialect was bad and I could not understand what he said. He got very annoyed and said, 'You speak German; so I will speak in German'; but I still said that I did not understand and he got more annoyed and said, 'Concentration camp for you,' and told two guards to take me to prison.

It was quite by accident that they found Ted a week later,

but the question was, who 'shopped' me? Later on I was told by Karl Schneider that someone had put a note under Hauptmann Blumm's door, informing him of my whereabouts.

CHAPTER EIGHT

MY FINAL ESCAPE

EARLY in April, 1944, I started making fresh plans for my escape. I decided I was going to escape the same way as I had done once before. There was an enormous amount of detail to be gone into. Firstly Schneider had to organize it so that Wally Whitehead, with his party, could come into our camp at a certain date and certain time, for me to change places with Wally. This time it had to be a complete change of people. I was to become French and he was to become English; as I have said, he was a Scotsman. He was to have my Stalag disc, all my Red Cross parcels, all my letters and all the other bits and pieces that came through and I was to go into the French camp with his Stalag disc, etc., etc.

The French soldiers had to go out to work; they were not of rank that the Geneva Convention controlled as non-workers and each day two parties of French workers used to go out and work at the quarry, breaking and digging up stones for roadways. The work was hard and they did a 7 a.m. to 1 p.m. shift. In the afternoon the other party of Frenchmen would go out and work from 2 till 6. Plans had to be made as to which was the best shift for me to go out with, what I was going to wear, where I was going to hide my escape equipment, and so on.

The first two items that I had to acquire were garlic and as much pepper as I possibly could because part of this working party was controlled on occasion by civilian guards with dogs and it would be necessary for me to use pepper and garlic to take away the scent once I had started to escape. While I was away on my previous excursion, cigarette parcels had come from England and, as I had stopped smoking, I was able to barter my cigarettes for pepper, chocolate, cocoa, coffee and soap – everything I needed to make black market with the Germans, and I was sure that it would be necessary to do a lot before I reached my objective. I needed contacts. The first person to contact was the Hungarian tailor in the French camp because he had to make me a civilian suit. He was the man who had made one for me when I did my trip dressed as a German NCO and he still had my measurements but no material. I managed to get another RAF greatcoat, and he managed to get me a pair of French trousers. I had good boots that had been sent out to me for my previous escape, which had come from England in a Red Cross parcel. I had a RAF shirt and the Frenchman made me a tie which would match the shirt. These French PoWs could get nearly everything; they used to do business with us in the British camp and then go out on working parties and meet civilians; so there was a three-way traffic. It was not difficult to get garlic and I had no difficulty in getting a vast quantity of pepper. I had a new German identity card made for me by the New Zealand Sgt.-Major. I still have it today, and it really is a work of art.

The next thing that I had to get was something to carry all my goods in. Quite by accident I arrived at the solution – to steal Hauptmann Blumm's briefcase. But how was I to do this? This was another task that took me a couple of days. I had to watch my friend Blumm and his habits. I found that he came into camp between eleven and twelve every day. He would go to the British Camp Commandant and then he would go to the cookhouse. He used to come in an old Opel car. I did notice that he left his briefcase in the car and I thought, my goodness, I'll have that! So I lay in wait for him one day and, when he went into the cookhouse, I pinched his briefcase. I took it to the lavatory and had a look to see what he had inside it. I was rather hoping that there might have been some papers in there that I could have used, but they were no help to me whatsoever, just details of requisites for the cookhouse and standing orders for his guards; so I bundled all these papers together, tied them with Red Cross string and took them to our 'Man of Confidence's' hut and handed them to a corporal in there. I told him that I had found them outside and didn't know to whom they belonged. When Blumm came out from the cookhouse he went stark raving mad. His briefcase had been stolen. He went to Sgt.-Major MacKenzie and nearly tore the place to pieces. Later MacKenzie sent for me and said, 'You brought some papers into the office, Beeson. Where did you find them?'

'They were found down the lavatory,' I said. He then said, 'Did you steal Hauptmann Blumm's case?' and I said, 'Oh no, I didn't.' It was a terrible lie and I didn't like to lie – not to our English folk – but I needed that briefcase so very badly because that was the last part of my outfit which would make me look like a German in every detail. I kept it and I have it at home today. Hauptmann Blumm retaliated by stopping the issue of letters and Red Cross parcels and this went on for a few weeks. I think people really thought I had stolen it, and of course they were right. I wasn't popular at all. That was fair enough, because not everyone wanted to escape and not everyone could. I appreciated their point of view – they were quite entitled to be a bit narked about this. Nevertheless I wanted to get back home. As a soldier it was part of my duty to get back.

The day of my departure from 383 arrived. Wally Whitehead came into the camp and went to the lavatory where I met him and we exchanged greatcoats. I walked out of the camp on the afternoon of 1st May. Wally was to sleep in my bed and to hang my disc on his arm and he was to pretend to be asleep when the German officer came in to check the Stalag disc numbers and the number of persons in the hut. So all they had to do while Wally was asleep was to look on his arm and read the number of the Stalag disc. All he had to do was to grunt and groan. They came in and checked him and there were hearts in people's mouths but luckily enough they never guessed that it was Wally. The

German guards went out and were satisfied. In the morning at 6 a.m. the guards came into my hut again and the boys in my hut emphasized to the guard that 2225 was *krank*, meaning that he was ill, and that he was not going on parade. This worked all right. Wally stayed in bed while he was identified.

I started out to work on the seven o'clock party to do a reconnaissance to see where I was going to 'jump' from, what obstacles I had and, how many guards there were. Also to get some escape gear out. The French boys were all very co-operative as they knew I was going to escape and before going out on the afternoon shift the French senior NCO agreed with the others that they would string our column of workers out gradually so that the column was very long. This gave the line extra length and made the distance between each German guard much longer and would give me a greater opportunity of getting away without being seen if possible. Certainly there would be fewer Germans to shoot at me.

As I went out with the afternoon working party an amazing thing happened. As we walked up the road we had to pass the Commandant's office and outside this office there were about ten or twelve British soldiers, who were desperately ill, being repatriated. Two of them were men I had lived with for a long time. RSM Tommy Green – he and I were prisoners-of-war in Poland – and Major Brook-Moore. They were on their way home under the auspices of the International Red Cross. I marched past the two men but they didn't recognize me and it was quite by chance that, when I went to a rehabilitation centre after I got back to England, I arrived at Leeds University and the first man I bumped into was RSM Tommy Green of the Durham Light Infantry.

The afternoon working party was going to the quarry and had to go to a shed to get tools. I was to be the first one to go into the shed, because in the shed was all my gear, and I was to collect this and make a run for it. I had to choose my time carefully because I needed to get to the trees for cover and also I needed time for a German guard to pass a certain spot where he couldn't see me very well for a short period. I reckoned I had about three minutes to go from the hut to this small belt of timber. I ran and a German foreman saw me and shouted at me to stop. I still had my French over-coat and cap on and I kept running and running. The Germans fired several rounds at me but I got to the trees and continued on until I stopped for a breather. I had to take a breather as, running in a French coat and hat, I had got into a bit of a sweat. I took my uniform off and spread it with pepper. I rubbed garlic on the soles of my boots. It was now about three o'clock in the afternoon. I had to get holed up until it was dusk. So I walked backwards for a long way sprinkling pepper as I went along and I suppose I must have travelled altogether about two miles on this backward and forward walking expedition. I now had to stop because I was beginning to get near a clearing. It was a good job I did stop because, coming through some thickets a field away, was a boy with sheep. I went further inside the wood.

That was where I had to sit for about an hour and a half until the boy and his sheep had passed my position no more than fifty yards away.

I got my map and compass out from Blumm's briefcase and it would appear that I had about twenty-five kilometres to go before I arrived at my first destination which was Neumarkt. I couldn't travel yet as it was too light and it was going to be about eight o'clock before I could move off; then I had to crawl for a long way because it was open country. Just before I got to the roadway, where there was a big ditch as the road was higher than the field, I heard a motor-bike. I lay down in the ditch and the motor-bike went by. I climbed up to see what it was and there was a German with a man in the sidecar. Undoubtedly they were looking for me. I crossed the road and got into the woods and by this time it was getting quite dark. I walked through this vast woodland and it rose uphill, and the moon had just started to rise. It was a most terrifying journey. I travelled for hours, walking towards the moon which appeared to be at the edge of the wood. At first when I saw it it was only very small, and the woods were not very light. But as I walked the shadows grew as the moon rose; the woods became lighter and it appeared the trees were getting bigger and I became terribly afraid. Owls flew in front of me; occasionally I saw a fox or sometimes a badger and my heart was in my mouth every time a twig snapped. I wondered when the hell I was going to get to the end of this wood; I had walked for hours and hours. The distance to the edge of the wood didn't seem to get any less but the wood got brighter. However, I continued my journey and got to Neumarkt eventually next day at 7.30 a.m. I tidied myself up with dew from the grass and I had a small hand towel and a little bit of soap – just enough to keep myself clean and refreshed. I had to go to the offices of the council where there was a Belgian, in charge of all the office workers – most of them being conscripted labour. He was my first contact. He took me to his billet, where I rested for three days and he fed me. I was tired because I had been travelling for twenty-five hours and I had been walking for sixteen and a half hours with hardly a break, except while hiding. On the third day my friend went to the railway station, bought a ticket for Feucht. It was at this station I was to meet another Belgian who was the station-master there. It was only a small station, so I got there unhampered. The Belgian fed me and I lived in the attic of the railway station.

I bought a ticket and travelled by passenger train to Nürnberg, and I found myself in the marshalling yards at Zollhaus, where I found a goods wagon for Metz. I decided to wait for dusk before entering this wagon. Dusk came and I crossed the many lines to where the wagon was, but on my approach to it I was halted by a plainclothes policeman, but managed to get away from him by hitting him so hard under the jaw that he fell down and by dodging in and out of the empty wagons. I returned to a small wood where I had been hiding, slept the night again and the following day caught the 4.55 p.m. train to Würzburg, arriving at about 9 p.m. The conversations between the Germans on this journey were very interesting. The bombing was certainly playing havoc with their morale. Everyone talked of casualties and damage – how they found it impossible to get things replaced. One woman from Ansbach related a story of how two German Air Force boys prevented a crowd of women from killing an American pilot who had dropped by parachute. There was an argument between two other women – one wanted the window down and the other wanted it up. I remained one night at Würzburg and how cold it was. I caught the 5.40 to Mannheim and arrived at about one. On buying the ticket at Würzburg for Mannheim, I was asked by the official why I was not travelling by *Schnellzug* and I replied that I had to receive orders further up the line regarding my work at Mannheim and this was accepted.

What a wonderful change in scenery as I travelled through the Neckar Valley – it is certainly a beautiful country. I changed trains at Heidelberg and had time to walk around this beautiful town. On my arrival at Mannheim I was surprised to find what great havoc had been caused by our bombers. I came out of the railway station and walked along the road and I looked for somebody to ask where the French prisoners-of-war and French conscripted labour was working. I asked one old lady and she said she didn't know. I walked on and then found another elderly lady and I said, 'Can you tell me where the French prisoners-of-war are working,' and she said there were no French prisoners-of-war there, but there were civilian Frenchmen working for the Führer at the Post Office sorting place. I asked where that was and she said, 'It is in the abattoir.'

When I got there I saw a Frenchman with a jovial face and I put my arms around him and kissed him in true French style and I said, 'I am an Englander – an English PoW.' I then said to him, 'Pretend you are my cousin.' He made a fuss of me and his name was Camus. (I have just had a letter from Camus's wife and he is very ill with cancer in Paris.) In all there were seventeen young men in this party, and the German officer came to me and said, 'Who are you?' I said, 'I am a Belgian, and this man is my cousin and I have just come to see him. I am working at the station, and I have had permission to come and see him.' He accepted my word. I stayed talking with Georges Camus all the afternoon and then when their work was finished I went with them to the place where they lived – one great big room. They got me some soup and bread and the usual coffee. They told me all about the war and what was happening.

All round them was completely demolished and they were living in one room of a great big house that had been shattered. I stayed here with these boys for three days and I had to make a very hurried departure, because a Gestapo man came into the room one evening and said, 'Where is this other man working who is with you and living with you?'

Camus said, 'There is no other man with us.' He counted and made seventeen, because I had seen this man coming and managed to make a dive for it down into the basement; fortunately he never came down to look. When he had gone, Camus came and found me and gave me addresses of where to go. The second night that I had stayed with these boys I had quite an experience. The sirens went and the RAF were paying us a visit. So we all went down into the air-raid shelter which was constructed in the basement of a six-storey building that had been damaged by blast.

The next day, while going to the station, I saw a party of young boys headed by their Führer writing on the walls, 'We shall never capitulate, never again 1914–1918. Our Führer leads, we follow. The Englishmen will have to pay the devil.' It was a nice feeling to see the Germans with their tails down. Mannheim was flat and out of action. After my speedy departure from my friends I caught the 8.05 p.m. train to Strasbourg, arriving at about 11.30 p.m. I walked out of the town and slept again in the fields. I was lucky – no one asked for my papers or anything. The next day I caught a tram-car that took me twelve kilometres out of the city where I caught a bus for Saverne. Here I was to travel two kilometres out of the town and go into the forest and find a house where the forester lived. I found this house with a little difficulty and introduced myself. I said that Maurice, their son, who was a prisoner-of-war in the French camp where I had just come from, sent them good news of himself; they were so pleased to see me.

They gave me a meal. Madame prepared a special dish and it was venison and for dessert we had cherries which had been preserved in cognac and that was a very wonderful dish. For our coffee I gave them a packet of English coffee and they were very pleased with it. They set up three cups and we had our coffee. We had only just finished drinking when the German forester called. He was the man who was in charge of all the forest around this area and they made me go upstairs into an attic very quickly and hide. He came in to the house and did his business and did not notice there were three cups on the table. As soon as he had gone, my friends came to me and said, 'Quickly you must go – but before you do we will give you an address where you can get help.'

The address that these people gave me was that of the lock-keeper on the canal near Saverne, which goes right up to Ostend. The forester said that he thought this man would be able to hide me on one of the barges. So I travelled to the lock and waited until it was dark.

I went to the house where the keeper lived and asked him if he could help me, as the forester suggested. He said that if I had come the previous week, yes, but last week he had got men on a boat and they had been captured and his son, who was in command of the barge had been taken to Germany and he could not afford to take another risk, but he gave me some instructions as to where to go and how to find my way and the kind of people that I would meet over the border, as I was now nearly on the borders of the old Alsace-Lorraine and France. He explained to me that it was going to be a very arduous task crossing these mountains and I can assure you that he never underrated that. By his conversation it would appear that I had five or six days to travel and the only ration that I could afford to eat was seven lumps of sugar a day, plus a little cognac that I still had.

The first night I walked up the thickly wooded slopes and when dawn came I was already very tired. I found a box bush, crept inside, broke off twigs and branches and made myself a bed. It was then about 6 a.m. At about 11 a.m. I woke up horribly cold and cramped. I came out into the open and did some exercises to get my circulation working properly. Suddenly I noticed with surprise, about a hundred yards away in between some thick clumps of pine trees, a house. At that moment two men came out of it and started to walk in my direction, so I dopped down quickly under cover again. As they passed I realized they were French. I stepped out and beckoned them to come over. 'I am English,' I told them, 'and I escaped from a prisoner-of-war camp and I hope to cross the frontier. Can you give me any details about it?' I went on, 'How far is it from here, and how closely is it guarded, and lastly, Monsieur, I am famished. Can you spare me a little food?'

They seemed scared, but then came close and spoke in low tones. They were conscripted workers and knew little about the frontier. They were strictly controlled. Food, unfortunately, they could not provide for they themselves were fed at German headquarters. 'Where are the headquarters?' I asked anxiously. They pointed to the house in the pine trees where they had just come from. 'There,' they said, 'are the area section quarters of the frontier police and you must beware because there too are the homes of their twenty-five patrol dogs.' They seemed to think that under the circumstances I should have little chance of escape. My only hope, they warned, was to lie low where I was until darkness.

The conversation only lasted a few seconds and they hurried off to their work felling trees. I fully appreciated the position of these men and that there was nothing they could do to help me. Indeed I was grateful for the silence which I felt sure they would keep. It would have been so easy for them to denounce me and receive the nice reward for the capture of an escaped prisoner.

Now I had a long and alarming period of waiting and I prayed for my good luck to hold. As I waited for dusk I became aware of how frightened I was. I prayed for my good luck to hold, for I knew that Dachau awaited me, or worse, if I should be caught again. It did not bear thinking about with the frontier to freedom so close.

For eleven and a half hours I kept in my hiding place, watching and listening for possible danger. Many times I saw the police coming in and out of the house with their dogs and I thanked God that I had been prudent enough to rub garlic on my boots to cover my scent. Undoubtedly the dogs crossed my trail frequently during the day, but at last dusk came and I was still secure. Finally at 11 p.m. I felt it was safe to venture out. Crossing the road which led to the house, I headed straight for the dense undergrowth. At first I was determined to climb the mountain in the dark, but after an hour's effort, I realized that it was too dangerous. The branches of the trees cut my face and many times I stumbled over, wrenching my ankles. Now I had been four days without food and the most foolish things got on my nerves. An owl flying across my path scared me stiff. The calling of the dog fox to the vixen sounded eerie and ill-omened.

Scrambling up that lonely mountain in sheer blackness made me dream of warmth and food and a comfortable bed and I was conscious as I had never been since I made my first dash from the working party in Poland, that I was near the end of my tether. I found shelter under a fir tree, and went to sleep. Just after three I was awakened by some animal which was on the prowl near me. I opened my eyes and saw two yellow eyes peering at me from a few yards away. I banged my fist on the ground over and over again until the animal scampered away. I wished I could say that I kept calm throughout my escape, but this lonely night shook me quite a bit. I felt terribly tempted to eat my last bar of chocolate but got over that by sucking half my day's ration of sugar. Then I began to climb again.

After about an hour the going became easier. The undergrowth cleared and gave way to rocks and huge pines. I watched the deer, fascinated by their leaps from crag to crag and it was a relief to see them about for it told me that human beings were scarce. I reached the top of the first spur but there were still two more ahead of me, each with its mountain stream which gave me beautiful cold drinks. At last, about three o'clock in the afternoon, I caught sight of the rough road along the summit which marked the frontier. There was little protective cover but I crept forward to a thick bush and from there watched the movements of the guard with two dogs. He was coming in my direction and I was alarmed at the speed of his approach. It was easy enough to conceal myself from him but I feared his dogs. The smell of garlic on my boots must have worn off by now and I had no more. I had been a fool to get so close to the road, but I could not turn back for this would have meant a dash across an open stretch of land with only the slenderest shelter to screen me. The guard and the dog came nearer and I sweated with apprehension. My luck held. A little group of men were felling trees by the side of the road and he paused to chat with them. I watched closely, waiting to leap across the road to the nearest cover on the other side, but he was still facing in my direction. Minutes passed and then to my intense relief he turned back and continued his patrol up the road in the other direction. I could just make out another guard on the road, but he was too far away to cause me any immediate trouble. I paused a moment or two longer while the nearer guard and his dogs got slowly further away, and then I slipped across the road into France. I had no idea of the best way down the mountain on the other side, and as I was almost done in I looked around immediately for signs of any solitary French person who might help me. Not far off was a little house.

When I got to it I found it was empty. I decided to work myself round to the rear of the men who were felling trees as I desperately needed rest and food. I knew that I must look haggard and bearded and my clothes torn and dirty. I dared not go far without cleaning myself up. I had to take the risk that these men were French and friendly.

Creeping up on them from one heap of chopped-off branches to another, I got within hearing distance of them and from their conversation decided that they were safe. I approached them and said to them, 'I am a British soldier and I want help.' I then asked, 'Can you help me?' I was lucky. They gave me a mug of funny-tasting coffee and directed me down the mountain to a small road along the side of which ran a narrow-gauge railway, which would take me to Cirey. I followed their directions and after walking about seven kilometres I encountered my first real helper, a middle-aged French woman. She caught up with me from behind, for by now I was crawling along at a snail's pace. How long she had been following me I don't know, but she must have noticed my condition for the first words she said to me were, 'You are English.' I looked at her eyes and they looked compassionate and trustworthy. I said to her, 'Yes, madame, I am English.' I told her my story and she simply said, 'Follow me. If you lose me, go to Café des Amis at Blâmont, a little village not far from Cirey.' I had meant to go deeper into France before asking for casual assistance, but I was so worn out that I thought with resignation I must take this chance. I couldn't go on without rest. If I was in bad hands I was finished. All was well. She took me to her little café and house at Cirey, and there I met her mother, a charming old lady who bustled me into her kitchen, gave me a drink of hot milk and then made me take off all my clothes for her to wash them in the sink. I was filthy dirty myself. My clothes and my body were dirty and I stank to high heaven. I washed and it was a joy to be clean. The two women had a terrible time with my clothes which were hard and sticky with sweat and grime. The daughter brought me a dressing-gown and cooked me an omelette and I dozed in the chair. When I had eaten I implored them to let me assist with the washing but they would not let me. The old lady took me upstairs and made me sleep in her own bed – white sheets, the first I had slept in for four and a half years. I rested my head on the soft white pillow and all at once an absurd thing happened to me – I started crying. I could not stop myself and I just fell asleep crying.

In the morning the old lady told me that her grandson was a prisoner in Germany. The two women had helped many airmen who had made forced landings to find their way back to England. 'We do what we can,' she said. 'It is not much.' But I found that they had all the arrangements beautifully organized. As soon as I had eaten they asked to see my identity card and other papers that I had on me. These would not do for France, so they made arrangements for my photograph to be taken and new cards to be made. During the day they told me that I was to catch an early train the following day to Paris, changing trains at Lunéville and Nancy. Then go by underground to an address where they assured me I would be in good hands. They were careful to give me very precise and detailed instructions because I could hardly make myself understood in French at all. Many years ago at Aylesbury Grammar School my French mistress had struggled to impress on me the usefulness of the French language but, alas, in vain. Although I had studied hard during the last two years of my captivity it had been wholly in German. I hated to say good-bye to these dear souls who had made my dream of escape seem more like reality; but now that I was clean and rested I felt full of vigour and keen to be on the move again.

CHAPTER NINE

FRIENDS IN FRANCE

THE journey to Paris went without hitch and the evidence I saw of the accuracy of our bombing interested me immensely. The marshalling yards at Bar-le-Duc, Châlons-sur-Marne and Paris were in a terrible mess – locomotives, coaches, wagons and rails were all twisted and standing edgeways against the sky. Many of the sheds were completely smashed, with rolling stock lying crushed beneath the ruins. It was a most impressive sight which made me realize that our bombing of strategic targets was much more effective than I had thought possible. Two French people spoke to me in the underground in Paris. I answered them in German as I had been advised to do by the women at Cirey. The address to which I had been directed was on the top floor above a little café in which an elderly woman lived alone. She was very poor. Her only son could not support her because he himself was an escapee and in hiding somewhere else. It was a tiny flat, just two rooms, a bedroom and a kitchen and there was only one lavatory for the whole building. The privations of the life here made me admire her all the more. This woman had an indomitable spirit. Gas and electricity were strictly controlled – switched off at the main during most of the day, so that the washing which was her only source of livelihood had to be done at a public wash-house. During the first afternoon that I was there she managed to collect five hundred francs for me at the wash-house.

These five hundred francs that Madame Pillar had collected for me must have been a great effort on her part. She was about sixty-five, a very small woman about five foot two inches and I don't suppose she weighed more than about seven stone. To collect this kind of money from the type of people who used the communal wash-house to earn their living was an outstanding effort and my thanks still go to them today. After the war I went back and spent a couple of days with Madame Pillar and she was so pleased to see me and we both had tears in our eyes. I will say once again, 'Thank you Madame Pillar.'

On the second day I found that she was feeding me from her own coupons which were not enough to feed her properly, let alone me as well, so I decided to move. The woman who ran the café downstairs, Madame Redin, knew of the position and asked me to live and eat with her. This I did, but they insisted on locking me in a room upstairs from seven o'clock in the morning until nine o'clock at night. Owing to my lack of French, I could say little to these people, but I tried to make it clear that I was anxious to get in touch with British Agents or some other means to continue my escape to England. I could not endure the prospect of continuing this sort of life indefinitely. They indicated that all would be well, and that I must leave the arrangements to them and I had no alternative.

I had not long to wait. After three days, details came through for my evacuation to Lille, where apparently my prospects would be brighter. I was taken to a café opposite, at the Gare du Nord, and there I met my agent. She was a young French girl, twenty-four years old, very attractive and petite, and possessing more courage, as I later found out, than any person I had ever known. About half-way through the war this girl, Marie Paule Tassart, who lived at No 37 Rue St. Pierre, Marq en Baroeul, near Lille, asked for leave from the managing director of the big cotton firm at Lille. The manager's name was Mr. Swan, an Englishman who had settled in France, married and had children after the First War. She asked permission to take leave and work for the Resistance. Her assignment, and her mother's, was solely the collection of allied personnel, whether they were RAF, sailors or soldiers. They set up organizing machinery for getting the soldiers, sailors and airmen back to England. Later on in my story, I am going to talk more of Marie Paule Tassart and Madame Tassart because there are definitely, to my knowledge, eight men who but for them would be dead. Marie Paule had already bought the tickets for our journey from Paris to Lille, which was a very exciting one.

The train, like all trains in France at that time, was packed to suffocation and I literally mean that. After a series of stops caused by allied bombings we were suddenly machine-gunned by an RAF plane which had been hedge-hopping. The gunner had been well briefed, for his bullets struck only the front three coaches which were restricted to the use of German soldiers. Soon after the train stopped again. I was wedged near a window and was one of the first to catch sight of something which gave me somewhat mixed feelings. Two RAF planes were hedge-hopping and these again were literally no more than ten feet from the ground and heading directly towards us. A few fields away a man was ploughing with two horses and as the plane passed by him the horses bolted across the field, dragging the plough behind them, leaving the poor old fellow sprawled flat on his tummy. Immediately he jumped to his feet and waved his cap in the air in welcome. That action was a symbol to me of the unquenchable spirit of France. Now the planes were roaring straight at our locomotive. All at once the train trembled and rocked and everyone started leaping out. I took Marie Paule by the hand and, pulling her through the confused crowd, ran across the field to shelter. I guessed the plane would come back soon to destroy the coaches. Glancing back I saw that the engine was completely smashed up. It was very amusing to watch the Germans. There must have been about four hundred of them scampering for cover and running for their dear lives. Not one of the officers took command to organize protection against the aircraft, although all the men were armed. For some reason the plane failed to return but we had to wait for six hours before another engine arrived complete with lifting tackle to push the other one over the bank. This line to Lille was a very important line. When the train was finally ready to start again, it was discovered that half the soldiers had run so far that they could not be found. The engine driver kept blowing his whistle and the officers fired their pistols into the air, before the stragglers could be induced to return.

But the excitement of that journey was not over yet. Just outside Amiens we stopped once again and watched the town being bombed. Afterwards we passed through the station and saw that it had been smashed to pieces by this previous raid. When we got to Arras the sight that greeted us was really extraordinary. A great crowd of Germans was on the plunder. Evidently there had just been a raid and men and boys were smashing windows and breaking down doors of the partly blitzed houses and helping themselves. We could see them clearly as they came out with their stolen goods. 'They are not our people,' Marie Paule whispered insistently. 'They are Boches.' Now as we watched they were in the gardens, wantonly trampling over the flowers and pulling up vegetables.

We moved on again, finally arriving at Lille, taking eighteen hours instead of six. It was 11.15 p.m. when we arrived and Marie Paule's mother, Madame Tassart, was waiting for us at the station. It was an uncomfortable walk from the station to her house for a curfew was in operation from 11 p.m. onwards. The streets were deserted and there was a great risk of being picked up by the German police.

I had spent two days with the Tassart's when the girl's uncle arrived and kicked up a fuss about my being there, saying it was too dangerous for the women. The women wanted me to stay but he had his way and my next host was a university professor, Professor Corsin, and Madame Corsin and their two daughters. Their home was by the side of the railway, high on the embankment. I was locked in my room most of the time but I was kept entertained by the many interesting people who came to the house. Some of them were connected with the Free French Forces of the interior, the intelligence section, for Professor Corsin was one of the chiefs. There was a radio transmitter under the railway bridge near by and the two Corsin children used to take messages for transmitting, pinned in the clothes of their dolls, causing great fear to their parents until they returned. One of the visitors spoke English well and spoke quite freely to me. 'You are the only person I can speak to without choosing my words with care,' he said, 'for I know there is not a soul to whom you could pass on this information even if you wished to do so.'

It was now early June and one evening he said to me, 'How you must wonder when the Allies will land in Europe.' 'Indeed I do,' I replied, 'but even more I wonder when arrangements can be made for me to continue my escape.' This was my continual cry for I was sick for home.

He patted me on the shoulder and said, 'You must be patient, but I will tell you something. Within thirty-six hours they will be here. We have received a message that the

107

colour of the mermaid's hair was changed and this is the code to tell us when the British will commence the landing in France.' As dawn broke, there they were amassed on the shores of Normandy.

One night when I was still in the house of Professor Corsin, I heard a lot of noise going on outside. I looked out of my window and saw an odd sight. About thirty yards away was the railway line and here a small train had pulled up. It was bright moonlight and I could see that four wagons contained medium and light anti-aircraft guns. There were four other coaches; two contained guards and two were of exceedingly luxurious types. As I watched, the guards took up their positions and there was silence except for the tread of feet and they literally closed the whole area with their patrols. I was becoming frightened as I didn't know quite what was happening. I guessed that it must be some high Nazi official lying up for the night. The sight of so many German guards so close at hand made Stalag 383 or worse seem horribly real again. Then I decided that my position was really rather comic. I went to sleep without undue alarm. The Professor and his wife, however, were evidently much alarmed. They came into my room at 6 a.m. and told me they were sorry but I must leave at once. They would send immediately for the uncle of Marie Paule. When the uncle arrived, there was a long conversation between the two men until the uncle suddenly turned to me and said shortly, 'Do you know your way back to Marie Paule's?' I replied, 'Yes, I think I could find that. I have only once been out on the streets since I was brought here, but I am sure I can find my way back.' 'Well you had better go there without delay and be very careful,' he said.

So I returned to Marie Paule's once more and I was not sorry for I had great regard for her. These were difficult times for any of the French who tried to aid the Allies and I could not blame the Professor for his nervousness. He and his wife had been very good to me, bearing in mind that the train that pulled into the viaduct just as you go into Lille station was none other than Rommel's own personal train, and he had stayed there for the night.

108

The next month was one of constant disappointment. There was a scheme to get me out through Belgium, but it came to nothing. There was a scheme that was to get me away by air, but after a week of excited anticipation we missed the plane by two hours. It struck me that the people I was in contact with had no link with the British Agents or Intelligence people who I felt certain were non-existent. I was greatly handicapped by my bad French and I hardly knew what was going on.

July came and my friends talked of my staying in Lille with them until the British armies came but the advance in Normandy had now slowed right down and I felt that it might well be many months before I was freed in that way, while the longer I stayed the more chance there was of my being captured and the situation for the Tassarts was also very hazardous for they could be picked up at any time by the Gestapo and shot, and tortured as well. Indeed I had already had many uncomfortable moments in Lille. One afternoon when I was in a queue waiting for a tram, a plain-clothes German policeman demanded to see my papers. He scrutinized them and looked up at me sharply, 'You come from St. Quirin,' and I agreed. 'Do you know that district well?' he continued. 'I know Cirey and Lunéville very well.' He went on, 'Ah, beautiful is it not?'

I smiled and said, 'It is indeed beautiful, but Paris and Lille have advantages.' He laughed cautiously at me and said, 'You are right, my friend. This nation has lost everything except the art of entertainment.' He looked at me and he looked at Marie Paule. I didn't learn French at school very well, but I was certainly able to hold my own under normal circumstances with any German.

Marie Paule had been given the name of an FFI (French Forces of the Interior) member in Paris. It was his job to do sabotage in Paris and to get Frenchmen who had been caught away into hiding and then into the Resistance, and it was decided that we would go and meet this man, called Kiki. Now came the problem of transportation and of money because all the savings that Marie Paule had and a lot of her mother's money had gone. So we had to go to friends to borrow money to enable us to accomplish this mission. From various friends, and including two thousand francs, the last money that Marie Paule had, we acquired ten thousand francs. For the last month there had been no trains from Lille to Paris and we had to make plans to go by lorry. This was to take place on Tuesday, 15th July, but we had to postpone it until Thursday, and thank God that we did because the vehicle we would have travelled in was smashed up by British planes when they were road-strafing.

The journey from Lille to Paris was not very pleasant. The lorry broke down many times and we had to ride high up, about eighteen inches from the roof on a load of freshly picked green peas. The journey took twenty-seven hours against the normal eleven, and what with the heat from the peas and the length of time of the journey, we were very tired by the time we reached Paris. We had two control checks for papers, one by the military at the Demarcation Line, meaning the area which was controlled by Marshal Pétain's *Milicien* on the outskirts of Paris.

The first check was quite interesting. Two German soldiers checked us and asked why we were travelling and I explained that I was on business and the girl said she was visiting a sick aunt. They did not realize that we were together. The next one gave me a fright – not because of my safety but because of the girl. The *Milicien* were worse than the Gestapo; one plainclothes policeman checked my papers and passed them. The other, an excise and customs officer, checked my case for contraband articles. He looked inside – all I had was a clean set of clothes. During this time I had not spoken a word. Then he checked the girl's case and found only clean clothes again. After putting two and two together he said to the girl in French, 'Ah, holiday making – very nice,' but she did not answer. Satisfied that we were in order he gave instructions to another customs man to enter the lorry and to ride to the destination and check the load as it was being unloaded, for arms. But we had none, of course.

During this journey, just after we had left Lens about twenty-five kilometres outside Lille, we picked up two other passengers who had been out black marketing, meaning that they go out into the country to farms and buy goods, take them back to the big towns and sell them for about twenty times the price that they paid. They had quite a load of tobacco and other items which were taxable and also forbidden. The *Milicien* searched these men and found the items and then arrested them. Other passengers during the journey were a *Milicien* guard, a French policeman with an arrested Frenchman and a German soldier. There were very hot moments during this journey which seemed to last many hours.

During the last part of the journey the customs man got into conversation and started flirting with Marie Paule. Thinking that we were out honeymooning he asked why we did not speak. The girl said I was deaf and dumb. After a while the girl gained confidence in this man after he had explained that he was FFI personnel and when we got off the wagon she said, 'Shake hands with an Englishman.' He looked at me and was so pleased to meet me and apologized for not being able to give me any tobacco but gave the girl some instructions where to get assistance. This was a shot out of the blue because we had nowhere definite to go once we were in Paris, except that we were going to find a man whom I had met while staying in Paris prior to my coming to Lille. This was a man who used to travel once a week to Normandy to make black market, and he was the man who got me drunk in his house on Calvados. I have omitted to state that the information that this FFI man gave us was to cost 5,000 francs each. So we had to find some more money when we got to Paris because our 10,000 francs had all gone.

First we went to the man, the black marketeer, and we stayed there for the night. He fed us well and gave us money. I think he gave us 8,000 francs, but I am not sure. Our next job was to go and find the Agent who was an FFI Intelligence Officer. Marie Paule got me to this rendezvous and we had the shock of our lives. It belonged to the man named Kiki and it was a brothel. We went upstairs and met Kiki and whilst Marie Paule was explaining to him a couple of his belles come up to me and started flirting with me. I never spoke to them – I was a bit scared – I didn't know what the situation was here because it said on the door *'Nur Für Deutsche Herren'*, meaning 'Only for German gentlemen'. Kiki came out to find me, told the girls to leave me alone and took me into his office. He said that at the present moment he had nowhere for me or Marie Paule to live. But he gave us money and said, 'You must find somewhere to sleep and I will feed you well once a day.' The address where we fed was Café Britannique, Rue Blondell, Port d'Arras. Kiki gave us a fair amount of money.

We came away from Kiki about 9 p.m. and we caught a train for Gare St.-Lazare. It was about 9.30 p.m., so we had to do some quick hunting for rooms. Marie Paule decided that the best place for the next two nights would be an hotel, President Wilson. We went in and looked at the room, furnished beautifully and not very expensive. There were very few people staying in Paris at this time and we decided that we would stay there, myself pleading deaf and dumb. My wonderful girl did all the necessary arrangements. One could obtain sleeping accommodation fairly easily but one had to be prepared for snap Gestapo raids. The real worry was food, for everything was rationed by coupons. We had to live on one meal a day, but we needed odd bits of food for something to eat in the evening and just an odd bit of bread in the morning. Marie Paule managed to buy some food coupons and that kept us going for the first two or three days. On the third day we ran out of food coupons and I suggested that we went to see the people that we had seen a few days previously and the place where I had lived for a couple of nights prior to going to Lille. I was greeted once again with tears and kisses by the woman and, with the help of my friend, explained what the position was. The woman said that she would feed us but lacked accommodation. This was good news as it meant that we did not have to make regular visits to the Café Britannique for food as we had enough money for hotels and we could journey backwards and forwards to our friend to eat. We changed our hotels every other day, that being long enough without the proprietors getting suspicious, because even in Paris it was difficult to trust people. This we did during the nine-days stay in Paris. Luck had now turned. I had met a counter espionage man named Monsieur Georges. He was a South American; he worked chiefly for the British but also did work for the Germans, and he once said to me if either Marie Paule or I were ever picked up by the Gestapo that I was to call him and to say nothing but that I would only answer questions that Monsieur Georges put to me. This was very heartening news.

Monsieur Georges was true to his word. He got information to Kiki and Marie Paule used to meet Kiki in one of the parks of Paris to get information of when we were to move and where we were to go. Not having found a direct means to Spain, we had found means to go to Perpignan or to Carcasonne. These places were where there were groups of FFI and Maquis. Days sped quickly by and on the fifth day after meeting Monsieur Georges, life became rather exciting, never knowing at what moment we were going to board a train and go somewhere. The Resistance were trying to get us through to Perpignan and Carcasonne but both these journeys failed because these routes had been broken up by Marshal Pétain's *Milicien*. Two more days went by and Marie Paule again met Kiki but this time had good news. We were to go to an organization at Toulouse.

We were both now feeling quite fit because we were feeding and drinking well.

On the ninth day we were ready to leave, having completed all the arrangements. Marie Paule went to the station to get travelling permission from the Germans and this took several hours. It was not an easy task to get these permits. We went to the station and waited in the queue to catch the train to Toulouse for three hours – but we were not on the platform. So I suggested to Marie Paule, 'Go up the front and see if you can bribe the ticket collector with a hundred francs,' which she did. Now we got on to the platform, but the next thing was that it was impossible for us to board the train, it being absolutely full; so my friend again bribed the attendant who was organizing the flow of personnel into the coaches, with another hundred francs and he made a lot of fuss and made the people move down and there was just enough room to get inside the door. It looked as if we had to get in and stay near this door all the way to Toulouse. We had been standing just inside the door of the compartment and nobody would move down – I don't think it was possible in any case – and a man poked me and I whispered to Marie Paule, 'Push tight against me.' I gave him a wallop in his stomach and as he bent down I passed by him and pulled Marie Paule along and we managed to get down into the corridor of the carriage.

We had been standing, packed like sardines, for about half an hour when I saw our friend Kiki. I told Marie Paule and she managed to push herself against the window and he came to speak. He explained that we must get out of the train immediately and meet in an hour's time at a rendezvous in a park. It was not possible to get out through the door so Marie Paule undid one of the windows, and we jumped out. This caused some concern among the occupants of the train and they wondered what the hell was going on, but we got out and walked along the platform and came out of the station. When we met in the park Kiki explained that we could not go to Toulouse as the organization had been completely smashed up by the Gestapo and that we must remain in Paris until he could find other organizations. I was very much against this, feeling that if we remained in Paris any longer we should be captured. Although I was beginning to feel quite at home in Paris, I felt that our luck couldn't hold for ever.

We met Kiki the following day and he said that we could go down to Lyons and his brother would be able to help us and so all the permissions of travelling and obtaining tickets had to be gone into all over again and it took four days for Marie Paule to get her money back and to have her work permit altered from Toulouse to Lyons. The date now was about 27th July, and the traffic system in France was completely disorganized. We arrived at the station six hours before the train was due to leave. We could not get on the platform as the train was already completely full and all the bribing that we had used before was of no avail. Many people came away from the queue and as they did so I managed to get our noses more forward.

While waiting in the queue I saw the two plainclothes German policemen watching the queue for likely victims. These men are easy to pick out. Always they stood or walked with an air of great importance looking down on people as though they were dirt. Generally they had short cropped hair and nearly always were the square-headed type.

Thinking that our hopes had gone for boarding the train, we were about to leave when the Germans must have found another carriage and shunted it on to our train. About three hundred people were allowed to pass the barrier. When the people got near the train and carriage entrances, I tripped one man up and as he fell, so more people fell on him. I took Marie Paule's hand and I pulled her and we ran along in front of the others who had fallen down, I suppose about a couple of dozen altogether. Some got up and punched some others and, while they fought, we got on the train. It was packed and in our two standing places we managed to get one of our portable chairs placed. What an argument Marie Paule had with another woman. This woman started pushing Marie Paule because she said Marie Paule had got her place, and that there was no room for a chair, but Marie Paule stuck to her guns. She plonked the chair down and sat on it. I stood beside her. What a companion. I would say that anyone whom she befriended could not wish for a better friend. They might come as good, but certainly never better.

Our train left about one hour later and had only travelled about seventy kilometres when it was forced to halt, because a group of Maquis had blown up part of the track and we had to wait about eight hours while it was being repaired. Then we moved off again only to halt again about a further

115

sixty kilometres. And the same thing had happened, only on a larger scale. The Maquis had waited for an ammunition train and had blown it up and there were goods wagons or parts of them that had been hurled yards away. This delay kept us waiting for nearly a day. By this time we were getting very tired. I made my friend as comfortable as possible, by sitting her in her chair, with me standing in front of her so that she could rest her head on my back. She fell asleep, poor girl – she looked lovely while she was asleep. She must have been very very tired because we had been on our feet for two solid days before boarding the train and what with this and the mental strain I know how she must have felt because I was feeling the strain too. She had been asleep for about three hours when she awoke and said, 'George, you must change places,' but I told her it was only half an hour that she had been there, and persuaded her to remain a further hour, which she agreed to.

Next to our chair there was a great pile of what turned out to be propaganda sheets. The young men who stood next to these pulled two large bundles down to sit on, and this made room for me; I kept my friend company by having a very disturbed sleep of about two hours. When morning came, my friend jumped out of the window along with many other men, took our empty wine bottle and went in search of water, to wash with and to drink. But we only swilled our mouths out. Marie Paule had enough foresight to bring a bottle of wine with her from Paris because it is not good to drink French water. She did not come back empty-handed and so we had a lick and a promise; it certainly felt good. I shall never forget her climbing back through the large window in the corridor. The train had been stopped because of the terrorist action and the window was high from the ground. It was impossible to pass along the corridor and get out as it was so packed. Many people were huddled on the floor trying to sleep. As my friend crossed the rails to our carriage, I put out my two hands and helped pull her up. She came in through the window like a cat. Very seldom would Marie Paule allow me to go on such errands because she

116

said my French was too terrible. A little later our train moved off, only to stop again at a small station just before Dijon, because Dijon was being bombed. We stopped here for about sixteen hours. It was becoming very difficult for me by now as the boys with the propaganda sheets had been trying to get into conversation. On the odd occasion I did answer them in German, but Marie Paule was always on the alert for such an occasion and she would take over. To keep the young men from worrying me, Marie Paule started to flirt and sing with them (she could sing beautifully and play the piano). This got her familiar with the boys, and she explained that I was a Dutchman with only a little knowledge of French, but that I spoke German. The next time the chief boy of the party spoke in German, and when I heard him speak I became very happy because his German was not perfect by any means. I think he was a Dutch Quisling. This relieved the situation and I could see the relief on my friend's face.

As we approached Dijon, we could see the beginning of the results of the bombing and also the work of the French Resistance. This was terrific. As we passed through Dijon, on the newly laid track, the damage was so great that I cannot find words to describe it. Dijon was apparently one of the main centres for the building and repairing of railway wagons and locomotives, but certainly it would never be used again by the Germans. The vast repair sheds and the timber-drying kilns were just a mass of twisted timber, and there were many wagons that had been blown to pieces. Just outside Dijon the propaganda boys and their German official opened the packets and threw a few leaflets out of the window, which the wind scattered in all directions. These leaflets were headed, 'You Catholics of France.' It was calling them to arms, to fight the Russians. This throwing of leaflets continued until we reached Lyons. At all the large towns and small wayside villages they threw out their propaganda. At Mâcon the train was searched by French *Milicien* and German Police for identification papers; I had to show mine but it passed without a query.

117

We arrived at Lyons three and a half days late, just in time to see the last train depart for Nice during the occupation by the Germans. We had an address to go to at Lyons. Once again it was a brothel and kept only for German officers, and the same type of large notices were displayed. The man that we were to see turned out to be the manager of the place. Near us there were several girls and two of them immediately pulled their dresses up to such an extent that it was very indecent. They started to try to attract my attention although I continued to talk to my friend. When the man arrived he spoke to the girls and said I was a friend of his and it was not necessary to continue with their business. After a chat and a drink he took Marie Paule and me away to his private flat, just a two-roomed affair with very little sanitary convenience. It was fairly well furnished and he lived here with his women. When I exclaimed that we were turning him out and that we could find two rooms at the hotel, he said it was not safe. So we stayed. He explained that we would have to remain here for three days while contacts were made for us to cross to Corsica. We should be alone, but he and his chief would call every day about 11 a.m. and bring us food and give us news of how things were going.

While we were at this flat, and I was away once doing my ablutions, he tried to have an affair with Marie Paule, and I challenged him about this and he said that it was not true, but if we liked we could share a room in the part where the prostitutes were. I said to Marie Paule, 'What about it,' and she said, 'Yes, it will be better there than becoming involved with this person.' So I told him that we would like to go and share a room in the other part of the building and he said that would be all right. It was a very large room, divided up in small cubicles, about twelve feet by twelve feet, and all they had in each of them was a bed and a chair.

All that separated the rooms was hessian which was tacked on to pieces of timber which made the framework. Luckily for us that night there were no activities as far as the girls were concerned. At least we saw none.

118

Marie Paule slept on the bed and it was a kind of a home-made affair – about three foot six inches wide and the basis of it was canvas held up by a kind of sprung mattress and on top of the base there was a kind of straw mattress about four inches thick – all lumps and bumps. We slept till about 5 a.m.

I said to Marie Paule, 'Do you itch?' and she said, 'Oh, I do.' I said, 'Come and stand up here. Let us go over to that window.' We went to the window and I said, 'Look, Marie Paule – look at these blasted fleas.' I took my trousers and shirt off – I had no vest – and I started de-fleaing like I used to de-louse when I was a PoW and Marie Paule took all her clothes off except her pants and we had got dozens of fleas on us. So I said that there was nothing we could do about it until the boss came back and when he came in at about 11 o'clock I asked him what the hell he thought he was doing poking Marie Paule and I in a place like this. But he said it was all right – no girls in there to worry us. I told him I would have preferred to see the girls than what we had then. I said, 'We have got so many fleas that you can hardly credit it.' He told us that they got fleas from the sand in the South of France – but I said, 'I think these must have crossed the Sahara as they are as big as camels some of them.' He said, 'Well, there is nothing I can do about it – this is the only place I can offer you. I will do what I said – I will provide you with food and get you away as soon as I possibly can.' We just had to accept that. Marie Paule still had some marks left and she used to go out in the mornings and buy some fruit and lettuce and radish and anything she could find to go on our bread. The man would come between one and two o'clock and bring us other food and in the afternoon we used to go down to a little canal and wash our feet and legs and that helped to get rid of some fleas, but when we came back at night we walked about practically naked except I had my pants on and Marie Paule had her bra and pants on. And that was how we lived for two or three days.

Arrangements were made and tickets were brought for us to go to Perpignan. We arrived at the station at Lyons quite safely after being collected by the chief and one of his agents. Having had a good meal and receiving a parcel of food to take with us, it was 11.30 a.m. when we arrived, and our train left at 12.15 p.m., so we found a quiet place on the platform and sat down. The train had not arrived by 12.30 p.m. and the loudspeaker said that it would not arrive until 3.15 p.m. so we went into the first-class waiting room to wait. About 3.30 p.m. the speaker stated that it was possible that no further trains would run to Perpignan, but they were trying to switch a train over to call at Lyons at 5 p.m. and that this would definitely be the last train to go to our destination. Just after 5 p.m. two men entered the waiting room – one leading the other by the arm as he wore black glasses, supposing that he was blind. He gave us this impression. This blind man was about twenty-four and the other about seventeen or eighteen. As soon as they entered the door the blind man took off his glasses and went to a man and asked for his papers. These men proved to be *Milicien.* I noticed this and left my friend and went over to the mirror and combed my hair, watching the men through the mirror, while they were searching the person's papers. I strolled casually out of the door and for the moment was safe. My friend, who was now quite alone, saw what was going on and she came out of the waiting room and went in the opposite direction and that is where we both waited for each other.

Now we were in a jam – no trip to Corsica, no trip to Perpignan, no trip to Toulouse. I sat down and my mind wandered back over the past six years. I had escaped in Poland, I had dug three tunnels, I had escaped twice into a French camp to find means of escaping but had been captured, I had cut barbed wire twice, escaped as a German NCO, and lost a plane to England by two hours. Where does a man's endurance end? What makes him still go on with extreme odds against him?

After leaving the station we walked across to a kind of a park and sat down. To stay in Lyons was absolutely hopeless and we decided to find a vehicle going south but we were unable to find one. We went back to the brothel and the man who owned it gave us an address of a lorry that was going south and said that the lorry driver knew of a group of Resistance men who would be able to help us. We met this driver and we proceeded on our journey south. We had travelled about 70 kilometres when we were stopped and a *Milicien* on a motor-bike pulled us up and stopped the vehicle and told the driver to get out and the driver said he wouldn't so the *Milicien* pulled a revolver on him and said, 'Get out or I will shoot.' So he had to get out and the *Milicien* wanted to know what he was carrying in the truck and wanted to get into the back of the vehicle. As we were in the back the driver wouldn't let him look. Then the *Milicien* threatened to shoot the driver, instead of which the driver took the pistol and shot him. Now we were in a real jam and we had no alternative but to throw this fellow into the ditch and take the motor-bike and hide it further down the road. We returned to Lyons; to continue was too dangerous.

On our way back the driver said that he knew of another group of French Resistance and that the chief of this was a French MP. He was sure he would be able to help us in every way. We had to remain the night in Lyons and meet this driver the next day. So we went back to the brothel yet again and had another night of flea-hunting but little sleep. We had some food and a bottle of wine given us and we had some food for the journey the next day. We went to the rendezvous to meet the driver. He was a greengrocer and had a shop at a place called Ambérieu which is a junction point for the railway going to Nice and into Switzerland. We had to wait a while. When he came he said that he couldn't make the journey because he had got some difficulties with his lorry. It was a wood-burning vehicle which has a gas-generating plant fitted to the side and it burns wood and that makes gas and the gas makes the engine go. But he had brought a friend of his along and he said that he would go to the station with us at Lyons and he would buy a ticket for me and Marie Paule would get her own ticket. And he did that. Ambérieu is fifty kilometres from Lyons. Little did I know that this man was coming with us. We had had so many frights that we wondered what was in store for us now. We had no alternative but to trust him. His remarks and movements seemed straightforward enough but nevertheless I was very apprehensive about him. Just before we arrived at Ambérieu the man called me to the window and both Marie Paule and I looked out together and he showed us the remains of a German supply train that the Maquis group, where I was going, had blown up and he said, 'Good work eh!' and I laughed, but wondered where I would finish up.

When we arrived we were taken to a café where we met the chief of the Maquis for that particular area. His name was Monsieur Quinsin and he was a member of the French Parliament. He took us to his château where he hid us for two days, while he made arrangements for a vehicle to take me to a hide-out of the Maquis high up in the mountains. During our walk from the station to the villa, he showed me two places where there were marks on the walls where the Maquis had fought a running battle with the Germans in the streets. He told me how, after the fights, the Germans had taken reprisals by rounding up men from their houses and shooting five for every German killed, but even this did not kill the spirit of the French. It was a dangerous walk as we were liable to be picked up at any moment and sure enough, my heart did come in my mouth once when two German patrol cars, mounted with machine-guns, stopped just in front of us. Nothing happened – we just walked by.

I was well cared for by Madame Quinsin (who was later to turn to me for help). The time came for me to depart. Madame got our lunch and we sat at the table but I could not eat. My little French friend was broken-hearted at having to leave me. She tried to eat her lunch but could not and then she burst out crying and ran upstairs to her room. In a mixture of French and English, I tried to console her and it was then that I suddenly realized how much she loved me. Just before I went, she picked a little leaf from the garden, kissed it and gave it to me and then pushed her tiny dictionary into my hand and said, 'Hurry, my darling, get into the lorry, the driver is waiting.' And as I climbed into the wagon I saw her throw me her first kiss as she ran away crying. In the small dictionary Marie Paule had written, 'I love you so much, my darling.' I still have the leaf that Marie Paule gave me. Now Marie Paule lives in England and has done for many years. She came to this country just after the war, married the brother of one of the RAF men she had hidden and lives at Bitterne, near Southampton. We have never lost touch. Her name is Mrs. David Richards and her husband has a motor engineering business. I went to her daughter's wedding and now Marie Paule is a grandmother, and I hope her grandchildren prove to be as good as Marie Paule, who is one of the finest and bravest persons I have ever known.

CHAPTER TEN

WITH THE RESISTANCE

WITH a heavy heart at having lost Marie Paule and seeing her go away in such distress I had to think now of my task ahead and I wondered what kind of friends I was going to meet. Truly the Quinsin family had started off well. They had housed us and fed us and Monsieur Quinsin had now got me on to a vehicle going to a small village called Tenay.

We arrived at Tenay with no incidents whatsoever. We pulled up at a shop and people must have known I was coming because there was a meal waiting for us and there was the chief of that area, a fine looking young man named Marcel Gaudet, and some of his officers. While I was having some food there, I had my first glimpse of the Resistance – there were about twenty men and they had rifles and sten guns and they were walking in file along the street of the village. These men were mostly young lads of about eighteen or nineteen and they looked very fit. They were men who had escaped from various German-controlled occupations and joined the Resistance Movement to fight under cover, day or night, whenever and wherever needed. I asked the chief, who was in the greengrocer's shop where I was having some food, what the men were doing – were they going out to fight a German patrol? – and he said, 'No, this village is always patrolled, both day and night.'

Tenay had only one street and all the houses on both sides of the road were backed tight against the mountains, just as though somebody had gone in with a bull-dozer and cut the sides of the mountains. On the south side of the village there was about a mile where you could actually see the railway track and that was where the station of Tenay was. Other than that it was just snug and tight among these rocks. If you travel into Switzerland, via Ambérieu, St. Rambert, Tenay and then Belley, you go then into the Haute Savoie and you are not far then from Switzerland. The chief had arrived in a Citroen car which had been converted into a wood-burner. Gaudet was about twenty-six with keen eyes and was a very business-like person. When I was introduced to him he was very pleased to meet an Englishman, but wanted proof that I was genuine, and the only proof I could give him was that I spoke English, but Monsieur Quinsin gave his word that everything was in order. So he accepted me and this man is now a very famous man, having done an awful lot for his country and having suffered.

Being satisfied that I was not a spy, we left the shop, got into the car and to my surprise in the back of it there were many sten guns and rifles, and four machine-guns. Also there were grenades, revolvers and ammunition. He told me to take a weapon in case we needed it because we were going a short way into a part occupied by Germans and one never knew when one might bump into a German patrol car and have to fight one's way out. So I took a couple of grenades. The chief's companion was a sergeant, a sturdy type of man, about five foot six inches and he looked a reliable sort of person, aged about twenty-one.

He sat in front with an Underwood repeating rifle across

124

his knees, ready for action. Now I realized that I was on my first mission, going to a disused railway siding where the Germans had had to leave a broken-down twelve hundredweight van. My new friend needed tyres, wheels and replacement parts and we were going to strip this vehicle. We entered the siding not even looking round to see who was about; we went straight to the vehicle and started work. Being an automobile engineer this pleased me and very soon I had a fuel pump, distributor, sparking plugs, water pump and coil off, while my friends were busy jacking up the van and taking off the wheels, and hunting for large stones to rest the van on so that they could release the jack as we only had one. We packed our gains into the back of the car. What a load! How that thing never broke down I just do not know. There was enough weight in there to break the springs and burst the tyres. It was a fantastic load. If we had run into a patrol going back, we would have had a rough time getting away.

We went back along the same way that we had come but just before the village we turned sharp right-handed and over the level crossing and travelled up the narrow mountain road for about half an hour, and until we reached a farm. It was a terrible ride – very steep, and at times very dangerous as we were liable to run off the road and fall over the steep sides – just sheer drops – and the hair-pin bends were the worst because we had to get out and push the car round because of the loss of engine power caused by running on wood gas. It was a frightening journey, more so for me because I cannot stand heights. I literally go all to pieces. I have no control of myself at heights. Also there was a danger of the car running backwards over the side because we had great difficulty heaving it round these bends with such a terrific load on, but the Maquis wanted this load badly as they were short of ammunition and guns. On the last trip, the aircraft which made deliveries had lost its bearings and dropped the ammo by parachute in the wrong place.

We came to the first plateau and in these mountains you

climb to great heights, and as you go up you come to a flat part where farming is carried on on a very small scale and some of the specialized cheeses are made here. There was always a welcome when you arrived at these places as they always wanted news of various people when you had been down in the village. There was always a drink for you – they would get the bottles out and some of their spirits that they made were quite potent – you had to be very careful – or I did as I was not used to drinking. I found some of their drinks a bit difficult to take and that is putting it very mildly. The poor old engine had a rest and we continued to climb, and we climbed for about another half an hour until we reached a peak where Marcel's headquarters were. We called some men over and they unloaded the car. We went away and had a drink and it was here that I was introduced to the NCO second-in-command. We had a chat and then he took me round and showed me the camp. This group was about sixty strong and the place was well fortified. They lived inside a big barn in which there was a haystack. But this was only a dummy stack. Inside it there was a small arsenal. The lower portion of the building had been reinforced with very heavy timber so, if it was necessary at any time to fight, there they had some protection. Then I went into the loft and here a radio for receiving and transmitting messages had been installed. Later I heard a message being transmitted to Berkeley Square in London, and this was to say that I had successfully escaped from a German prisoner-of-war camp and that I was now with this group high up in the mountains at Tenay.

Marcel was very keen for me to see all, but the first thing I saw that interested me was a kind of a hoist where the peasants lifted the oxen off the ground so that they could shoe them. It was like a big cradle with ropes which dropped down and went underneath the belly of the animal and this rope would be connected to a winch which was fitted with a wheel. They would turn this wheel – an old cartwheel – and this raised the ox off the ground so that they could shoe it. I have been connected with animals all my life and that was the first time I ever knew that oxen were shod. Up here with this group there were two oxen and one mule and the oxen used to haul ammo and various stores about from one place to another and we used to carry the rest ourselves. The mule had a very important task – I shall tell you about him in a minute. I next went and saw their stores – white flour, bread and home-made cheese – my gracious, I thought, what luxury – and the quartermaster said, 'Would you like some,' and I said, 'Yes please, I certainly would.' He gave me a knife and said, 'Help yourself.' I looked at him and he continued, 'Go on, help yourself.' This piece of bread was nearly the size of a pushbike wheel. It was hollow in the centre but the shape of a wheel and it was about eight inches wide so it was a wheel of bread. I cut a lump off this and the fellow didn't think it was enough and he cut me some more and told me to help myself to the butter. So I had a great lump of butter and then some cheese of the locality. Very similar to that of Gruyère. Can you imagine being starved after all those years and coming down and finding a haven like this? Being able to eat a big meal like this of bread and cheese – that was really something.

Then I went round the farm where they had just killed a beast and my friend explained that they were completely self-supporting. It was impossible for anyone to approach this part without being challenged. There were guards posted everywhere who had a complete view and command of the whole valley and each guard was connected to headquarters by a field telephone.

Now we had to travel higher and this time we had a four-legged companion and that was the mule. The mule's job was to carry food right to the peak of this range. He had all his harness, etc., for carrying two barrels of wine, one each side, and he carried everything that was required. I said to Marcel in my limited French, 'I am scared of this height.' 'Oh!' he said, 'there is no need to be, I will show you what to do.' He gave me the mule's tail and said, 'As long as you hang on to the mule's tail you will never fall down,' and he said that if I couldn't hang on to it to tell him and he would strap my wrists to it. And that was how I scrambled up these vast heights.

Now I said good-bye to Marcel Gaudet for the time being. I got into the captain's car and away we went. The captain explained to me that he had a lot of business to do because his group were off somewhere to raid a German convoy and he had received news that this convoy had been reinforced and was now too strong to be tackled by the original Maquis whose job it was and he had to catch them up and prevent a disaster. We caught them up after an hour's ride through the ups and downs of the mountains and there were five lorries full of French Resistance men and I should think, what with the cars and the lorries, there were about a hundred men in all. Each lorry had a machine-gun mounted on the cab and was ready for immediate action. These men were a fine looking lot of fellows, and I should think their average age was no greater than about twenty years. Each man carried either a rifle or sten gun and always four grenades stuck in his belt. But the action for these men for this day was off and they had to return to their camp high up in the mountains, while the captain and I drove round to various intelligence personnel for news.

I was now to see some country that I had never seen before. At one small farm the captain had to leave me and go to an intelligence officer and it was here that I had quite a fright. The Maquis boys were unloading some loot taken from the Germans. I got out of the car to stretch my legs and thought that I would go and have a chat with the unloaders. Apparently they had not seen me arrive with the captain and when I was about twenty-five yards away from them they noticed that I was a stranger, brought their rifles up to aim and I heard bolts go home as a bullet was thrown into the breech. Just then the captain came out and shouted to them and they put their arms down. Heaven only knows what would have happened if he hadn't come out just then. Jean Paul, the captain's name, told me to watch my step until I was known, for up here strangers were enemies until they had been proven otherwise.

128

We had to go to a small hamlet high up in the mountains and it was 12.30 midnight when we arrived. This place comprised one café, one church and about forty houses, facing a high and wooded mountain. The car was parked in a barn and the captain said, 'Now we start our climb.' It was a bright moonlight night. Nothing moved and nothing was heard except the occasional clanking of the cattle bells, fixed to the cows that were grazing on the mountain slopes. Our climb took us up a very narrow and rugged path and often we were hit in the face by twigs and at one place I had to put both my hands in front of my eyes to protect them, as it was so densely wooded in this particular part. At last we reached the camp and I was taken to my quarters – an old cattle shed, built of stones against the face of some great boulder. I was given three blankets and a place to rest my bones on the straw and there were other men sleeping and I was soon asleep myself.

I woke next morning at about 6.30, ate my breakfast – rye coffee with milk and sugar and bread and butter – and after breakfast I was issued with the Maquis uniform, boots, revolver, rifle, grenade and ammunition. After this I got myself acquainted with the camp, and I should say that we were about six hundred feet up above the first plateau where we had stopped. We had an excellent view of the whole valley. Truly this scenery was very wonderful and we could see on the other side of the mountain where the ups and downs had been straightened out. There were grapes growing on the lower regions on the slopes. There were small hamlets dotted here and there with dusty roads winding in and out and up and down these great heights. Cattle grazed on the lower regions and on the less wooded parts of the mountains. On the unwooded parts of the mountains there was corn cut ready to be carted and now and again we could see a Maquis lorry or motor-bike kicking up the dust as it went about on its various missions.

While I was sitting studying the country, the second-in-command came out and explained the whole area; seventy-eight miles to the east was Switzerland, fifteen miles to the

129

north was a plateau where aircraft once landed. This surprised me and I said, 'Once! Don't they land now?' He said they landed at the last full moon, but are unable to do so now as the Germans partly control this particular area. And so that was my hope of an early return home gone again. I wandered around the camp and found that it was spread over an area of about a quarter of a mile. Three tents were pitched among some hazel trees. Four others were quite a distance away among some silver birch and the captain's hut was built from logs and moss and the cookhouse was under some tall ash and chestnut trees. The NCOs' quarters was the old stone cowshed which gave us a full command of the valley. Here, through day and night, was posted a guard with a machine-gun. At the foot of the camp ran a road on which four separate guards were posted, that is east to west. One post was about a mile out and the other about half a mile. This applied to both directions.

The next day I went down with the boys to the curious little village – what a welcome I had. All the villagers wanted me to drink wine with them because many of these people had never seen an Englishman before as their life is completely spent on these mountains and they inter-marry and their outside world is a very small one. We talked about the war and what great praise they gave to Churchill and all the English people. It made me feel proud to be an Englishman and to realize that we were so well loved and respected. One lady took me to her *fromagerie* – gave me some milk and cheese and then cooked me some trout.

The next day the German aircraft were busy searching for us and they bombed a position about two miles away, thinking that we were hidden there. The next day they returned again and bombed, but this time they bombed a small village, killing eight people and wounding several more.

One night we received a message that a British plane was coming up to make a parachute drop to us; but somehow or other the Germans knew the details by picking up our code, and that it was coming the following night.

That set up complications and it wasn't very good for me

because they thought that I might be the one giving the information. I didn't know anything about this really – only heard a little about it. I made it my business not to know too much and when I spoke to Jean Paul about this he told me not to worry and suggested that we set a trap for this person. He said he had an idea and would need my help.

About a week later we had another failure. We were sent to a railway siding about twelve kilometres away to raid three goods wagons, loaded with Red Cross parcels that should have gone to prisoner-of-war camps but the Germans had pinched them. No sooner had we entered this siding when all hell broke loose and the Germans opened up with machine-guns and automatic rifles and there was no time to organize and everyone scattered. Later, some of us were able to get regrouped and a miniature battle took place and the Germans even sent a Messerschmitt over which sprayed the group with gun-fire with the result that we lost one or two boys. Later this little band of ours was to escape. We had three men killed and three wounded, but the Germans had at least eight killed.

We made a surprise attack on the stores where the Red Cross parcels were in the German goods wagons and we did well. We took our three lorries with us – that was all we had now – and there were only about a dozen German guards there and we shot all of them. We got the whole shipment of food parcels and supplies taken away and we also got another three lorries which we took from the Germans.

One of the necessities that we required was tents for us to sleep in and the SS had got some of these at their dump. This is where we had been to raid them and amongst the supplies that we took were tents. I had a German tent and I shared it with Maurice, the doctor. But on our way back from this raid, the Germans had set up an ambush for us and we ran smack into it. We took up our positions on the road and set up our machine-gun post and then we got round the back of these Jerries and by climbing up the slope of the hill where there were lots of pine trees, we dispersed these Germans and got safely back to our hide in the mountains.

131

The next day four prisoners were brought in – they were French – and apparently had been giving the Germans information about us and after a trial they were found guilty and shot in the back of the heads as traitors. But before they were shot they had to dig their own graves and when these were considered deep enough they were shot.

Many prisoners were brought in, tried and shot. As a general rule neither the Maquis nor the Germans took prisoners. I have heard some terrible stories of atrocities carried out on the Maquis by the *Milicien* and the Gestapo. One victim was a young Frenchman who had been found with his hands chopped off; another was a Maquis boy whose eyes had been dug out with a fork. When the Maquis boys fought they fought like tigers, expecting no quarter nor giving any and knowing what was in store for them if they were captured. The Germans also fought hard – but they often put up very little resistance. They knew what would happen to them if they got captured. If the personnel captured were *Milice*, Gestapo or SS they were forced to dig their own graves and then shot but if they were just ordinary soldiers they were shot and buried decently.

Referring back to the first Maquis chief, Marcel Gaudet, I think he was the bravest and most clever of them all. He loved his country and all his men and here are two stories concerning him.

News came through from his Intelligence that a train was due to arrive at Lyons at a certain time. He took twenty men, went to a point chosen by him, set his explosives, posted his men and waited. The train came around the bend, through the mountains, and this would be, I suppose, forty kilometres out of Lyons and when the train got to the point where the explosives were set, he fired. The engine and the four wagons went up in the air and finished up in the river bed about sixty feet below. He then went into action and killed the guards accompanying the goods train.

I think his master plan was when he destroyed two locomotives. His gang had destroyed a railway bridge on the line which comes from Switzerland into Lyons. They received information that a repair gang were on their way to fix up a temporary bridge. Again the train had to pass through the mountains. On the south side of the railway started the great slopes leading up to the mountains and this was wooded. Near the railway track on the right or north side was a small river, then the grass banks and the verge – and after that a small road. From the road upwards, coming towards the south again, stood some high rocks – and on these ledges were placed three machine-guns with their crews, while up on the slopes on the southern side, hidden away behind the trees other members of the Maquis were installed. Just in front of these positions two lengths of track had been taken up. The train came along, got to the spot and stopped. The Germans got out to replace the track and the Maquis waited for them to start working. When they were sure that all of them were out of the train, they machine-gunned them. The Germans scattered into the slopes, and this brought the rest of the boys down. Some hunted the Germans out and shot them while the others came down and blew up the train.

Marcel was lucky to be alive because about half-way through the war, he and about twelve members of his group were captured about 20 kilometres away from his village at Belley. They were taken to a bakehouse and down in the basement they were imprisoned. When the Gestapo chief arrived he had them brought out one by one, interrogated them and then shot them. It came to number thirteen and it was Marcel's turn. Marcel could run and jump like a deer. Instead of waiting to be interrogated he made one dive for it, jumped the wall, then a fence made of iron bars, ran through houses and managed to escape; and if you go through Belley and stop in the middle of the village where there is a big green, and look on the wall of the old bakehouse there is a plaque which says, 'To the memory of the Free French Forces of the Interior – twelve men were imprisoned, interrogated and shot here whilst their leader, Marcel Gaudet, with courage in hand finally escaped and lived to do much good work for his country.'

The Americans were now advancing up the Rhône valley and we moved our camp from the mountains. Things were not so dangerous now and this site gave us better scope if we should be required at any moment to go into action quickly. We were busy instructing recruits in anticipation of a big battle around Ambérieu but this never happened because the Germans evacuated the town with no trouble whatsoever. They just left the town in the hands of the Town Major.

One afternoon I was at a café and I had a couple of drinks with two elderly gentlemen when Maurice, the doctor, came in and challenged me to a drinking bout. He lined twenty-four glasses up on the table – twelve my side and twelve the other side. He challenged me to drink twelve glasses of wine to see who could drink the fastest. 'Good gracious me,' I said, 'I couldn't drink half a dozen let alone twelve!' He then said, 'You are a poor Englishman if you can't accept a challenge.' So, saying he couldn't talk like that to an Englishman, I agreed to have a go. We had quite a crowd, and there were three or four of the wives whose husbands were in my group of Resistance and of course they egged me on too. They said, 'Go on, Monsieur George, go on – beat Maurice.' So I started. I didn't beat Maurice but I did drink my twelve glasses of wine and I had nibbles of cheese as I went along. We all sat there talking for a couple of hours, and it was now about six. One of the ladies said to me, 'You come home and I will make you a special meal tonight.' I started to go home with her and other members of her family. I think they knew what was happening for when I got outside the café they stood each side of me to stop me falling over. They walked me to their house which was about a mile and a half away. They took me indoors and gave me some strong black coffee.

Having got me home safely they plonked me in an easy chair and I dropped off to sleep. They woke me about eight o'clock for a meal. There were a lot of people sitting beside a big long table. I don't know what this meal was, but it may have been a goose – I am not sure, but they got me up to the table and they served the food. Suddenly I had to run out to the kitchen; I felt so ill and was vomiting.

I washed my face in cold water and with that I collapsed straight on the floor. I wasn't wearing very much; I only had a pair of boots and socks, a pair of khaki trousers and shirt with the Cross of Lorraine on. They whipped these off and there I was in my birthday suit! This is what they told me. I did not wake up until nearly midday the next day and my goodness wasn't I ill. So ill that they sent for Maurice and he laughed like hell. Anyway they got me well and I went back to the mountains. Now I should never have known what took place at this party but for the fact that the first time my wife and I visited these people after the war, they told my wife the story and happily they told her, 'Oh, he is a nice big boy when he is undressed,' and my wife didn't know quite how to take it!

I had said good-bye to all the people at Tenay and promised that I would come back after the war, and this I did for about five years in succession and we are still quite a big family today. Although I haven't been to see them recently, we still write to one another.

I made my way to St. Rambert and said good-bye to various people and then to Ambérieu for it was now liberated and there was what was known as a Town Major in charge, a civilian. I went to see Madame Quinsin because she had lost her husband; he had disappeared. She had asked that when I came would I call to see if I could help her.

I went to her villa and she was all tears and so were the children. She explained to me what had happened, but I had been told by Jean Paul not to interfere with the domestic life of the French people – it was a question for the civilians to 'dive' into any business that needed investigation. I went and had lunch with her and she took me to the Town Major and I said that Monsieur Quinsin, the French deputy, had been a good friend to me and to another French girl, and he had helped me to get to the Resistance and I would like to know what had happened to him. I said it was suggested that he had been captured by the Maquis and had been taken somewhere and shot because he had been making black market with the Germans. If he had been doing this it was only to get information for us, because it was from the information that he gave us that one railway engine and goods train was blown into the river. He said there was nothing he could do at the moment but he would make some investigations. I was powerless to do any more and I stayed the night with Madame Quinsin. The Americans were only about twenty-five miles away then.

CHAPTER ELEVEN

HOME AT LAST

EARLY in the morning of the next day, there were crowds of people in the streets and it was obvious something was happening or about to happen and about eleven o'clock there came into Ambérieu's main street, a jeep and armoured car and three or four six-wheeled vehicles. I went up to the officer with outstretched hand: 'Shake yank, I have been waiting five years for this moment.' He said, 'Who are you,' and I told him and he said, 'That's okay by me – jump in.' I was up on that armoured car in a flash. I gave the officer in charge of the armoured car more information and he told me that they were the 171st Cavalry Regiment of the United States 7th Army and that their headquarters were in Rome. At this particular moment the General commanding this army was at Grenoble, so they sent a jeep back with me to a major who was backing up this advance unit. I told him my story and he said, 'All right, you must go back down the line in a convoy tonight and go and see General . . .' (I forget the name now). I got in this GMC six wheeler, but before I went I said to the officer, 'I need some food and clean clothes. Can you help me?' He said, 'Yes, go up to the PX wagon and help yourself.' I went to the 'buck' sergeant (about the rank of a staff sergeant in our unit) and said that I wanted food and some clean clothes and he gave me half-a-dozen pairs of socks, new trousers, new shirt, pants and vest, new boots and then detailed an American soldier to take me to the cookhouse and I had the shock of my life. They had there a great big portable oven where they roasted big chunks of beef and I had beef and potatoes, two or three kinds of vegetables and for sweet I had never seen such a big tin of fruit salad in all my life – it was a five gallon drum of Libbys and there was the equivalent in Libbys milk next door and all you had to do was to hold out a mess tin and I had it chockablock full of veg and beef in one part and chockablock full of fruit salad and cream in the other part. That was marvellous.

The next morning we travelled to their divisional headquarters and here I met Douglas Waugh, the correspondent for *The Daily Telegraph*. They greeted me extremely well there and so did Douglas Waugh. As a matter of fact he was more than a help to me. Mr. Waugh gave me four hundred Senior Service cigarettes and I told him my story and he said that he was afraid that I might have to get home from here on my own. I had already given Divisional Headquarters all the information I knew about the Germans.

The Americans were advancing very fast. Nothing was going south. I was hoping to get to St. Maxime, the place where the Americans had landed in the south of France. Douglas Waugh said that, twice a day, there were despatch riders who used to come to 7th Army and take messages to the British who were a long long way away, actually in Corsica, but he said that if I started to walk on this main road, I would be bound to see one of these despatch riders and he would tell them I was on the road and to stop and give me a lift. I had a terrible walk, lasting nearly two days before I got a lift. All the transport, streams and streams of it were coming up from the south but nothing going down. However, the DR did pick me up and I told him my story and what I wanted to do. He said, 'All right, I will take you as far as I can', and we had been travelling for about fifty or sixty miles and suddenly he said, 'I know. Here is a chance. The Germans have all gone from the airfield at Cisteron and the American fighters are landing there. I will take you to this camp and see if you can get a hitch hike to the British.'

As we went along I saw a large airfield on which we decided to try our luck. You can imagine my feelings when I saw many allied aircraft on the airfield. I went to an American Captain who was in the control tower and I said that I wanted to get a lift home and that I was a British soldier, giving my rank and number and told him where I had been. He said he was sorry that he was not allowed to give me a lift, or anybody a lift for that matter. I said, 'Well, that's pretty tough. Here are my papers. Here is my Stalag disc, and my French identity card. It is true it is faked, but I have been fighting for two years before you people even thought of coming into the war. We had half won the war before you people came in and now after all this time I have escaped from my camp near Munich. I have been in Poland. Don't let a chap down on his last lap home.' He then said, 'You have escaped from Poland and Munich?' I said, 'That's right,' and he grinned, 'Why sure boy, you're worth a ride; hop in that Mitchell.' I didn't know what a Mitchell was. There was only one plane near this tower and there was a Staff Sergeant there who the Captain had told me to look for. I went to the aircraft and said that Captain Clark was going to give me a lift to Corsica and that I was to get into the Mitchell which the Staff Sergeant told me to do.

So I got in and sat down and they put me where the wireless operator used to sit and he said, 'You realize that this plane is only a "communication" plane. We carry no guns so it means you take a risk if you come with us.' I said, 'Well I have taken risks for a long time now, so I will take a risk with you.'

Off we went and believe it or not but this was the first time I had ever been in an aeroplane, and we went to Corsica and landed there. I think the name of the place where we landed was called Bastia. We only stopped there for about ten minutes because he was a courier and he dropped his messages into the officer in charge and away we went. Next we landed at Rome and Captain Clark said he would hand me over to the British and just as he was getting out of the plane to go into the American quarters at Rome, he said, 'I won't leave you here. Come into the officers' mess and have a meal. It will be quicker for you to get home if I take you to Naples, because that is where the British Headquarters are.'

So we had a meal and off we went again and landed at Naples. In between times the Americans had radioed through to Naples and there were military police ready to take me to the headquarters and there I told them my story.

I was twelve days in Naples and during that time I had a really wonderful time. The Regent's Palace had been converted into an all-ranks Naafi. It was a marvellous place – all ranks could go there and there was always a full orchestra playing and the first piece of music that I heard being played by such an orchestra since I left England in 1939 was this string orchestra which played 'Come back to Sorrento' and it was so moving that I shed a few tears. There were drinks and you could get meals there – a most magnificent place. It was where the soldiers who were on active service used to come for a break. I also went to the Opera House but I forget what I saw but it was absolutely marvellous. I had a free pass to go there and I went to another theatre, I forget its name, but I thoroughly enjoyed that also.

The thing that made me very sad was when I walked round the back streets of the town and saw the people who were poor and saw how they lived. I shall never forget those sights – they were terrible. On the walls there were notices that the American soldiers had printed. It was in relation to prostitution that was taking place. There were some vile slogans on the walls and there were children, little girls from the age of fourteen years onwards, offering themselves. There were all types of women hovering on the streets. One thing we had to be very careful about was the stealing that took place by the Italians. They used to run behind service lorries and jump into the back and throw things out which

139

were of any use to them – particularly from the food lorries. They were daring enough to steal an Indian tent from our small encampment on the Bay during the night. The tent was about twelve feet square and made of cotton so it was possible for garments to be made from the material.

On the third day in Naples the boat left for England, taking home British soldiers who had been PoWs in the Italian camps. I could not go because I had yet to be identified. Naples had not received instructions from England for my clearance. I felt a bit sick about that and I saw the Commanding Officer. He told me not to worry and that I would be got home before they were, as he hoped he would get permission for me to fly. And this he did. On the evening of the twelfth day a message came that I was to pack my kit, not weighing more than forty pounds, and report in half an hour's time to the guard house where I should be transported to the airfield. If anybody wanted some real action they should have seen me preparing for this trip. I brought only a few odds and ends home. The rest I handed back into the quartermaster's stores for I was not going to be late for this journey. I waited at the airport until early morning and then the aeroplane left for Tunis, then Oran, and then Casablanca. What a wonderful flight that was, over the sea and over the desert. It was really a tremendous thrill. I had been in the air for about ten hours when we landed at Casablanca. I stayed at Casablanca that night and I had the VIP treatment all the time. Late evening I walked round the town and I was amazed to see how much greenery there actually was and the wonderful white buildings and palm trees. In the morning after breakfast we all had to assemble at a briefing room and there we were instructed on our various jobs that we should have to do should an emergency arrive. We flew from Casablanca to a secret airport in England in a Liberator. This was a special plane – it was fitted out with armchairs and tables and my companion sitting next to me was an American General and we talked and he was very interested in all my activities. He even went so far as to say that when the war was over would I go to America and he would find a position in his organization. I don't know what that was but I wasn't interested in going to America. I love England too much.

We landed at this secret airport, had tea, and within two hours I was on my way to London, where I knew my girlfriend and all my family were going to have such a surprise because they had no idea that I was on my way home. None of my relations had any idea what had happened to me and my father said to my sister, 'You will never see George again. He has escaped and they have got him this time.' My sister told me this but she did not believe it because Mary and I, right from the time she was a wee mite, had always been very very close together.

I arrived at Paddington in the early hours of the morning, having travelled all through the night. I then had to go to Marylebone to meet Intelligence Officers and from there I went on an underground train to Hammersmith. I caught a bus at Hammersmith Broadway and went to Chiswick Lane which is just off the Chiswick High Road and as I got off the bus I gave the conductress a penny and she said, 'What's this for chum,' and I said, 'I got on the bus at Hammersmith and this is my fare.' She then said, 'How long have you been away, mate.' I said, 'Since September, 1939.' She said, 'Here you are, mate, here is a shilling to go with it; you are worth more than that but that is all I have got of my own at the moment.' Apparently the fare was then fourpence.

I walked down Chiswick Lane and turned the corner and walked down Balfern Grove, and up at the window of her bedroom was my girl. She told me that she recognized my steps, and I remember her mother saying to me, 'Eileen heard your footsteps,' and she said, 'Mum, Mum, he is home.'

When I arrived at the house she was in her dressing-gown getting ready to go to work, but she didn't go to work, only along with me to go round and visit our friends; this would be September, 1944. That made it near enough five years that I had been away.

After my leave was up I went to Matlock and that was apparently an army school of rehabilitation and they nearly drove me mad there. I remember going into a classroom after being there about a week, and I had to pass an exam along with some other staff sergeants and they put me at a desk by myself with a chair and they gave me lots of discs of coloured cardboard and I just did not know what to do with them. Then they gave me some more coloured bits and these were in a form of a block, but I just didn't know what they meant or knew what to do with them. I couldn't do anything about it.

Then I remember in the afternoon they gave me a maths paper and by this time I was beginning to get pretty low. I rushed out of the room and went straight to a telephone box and I phoned Eileen and asked her to come up and stay with me – and I told her that things were going all wrong and that they had given me things I didn't know anything about with no instructions. I said, 'I am completely on my own, with no one to talk to and in a completely different environment than I have been used to.' And she came up and I sobbed and sobbed and sobbed. What I could not get over was that I had been through all my troubles having to use my brain and energy and all the resources that I had to get back to England and I thought that now they were trying to make 'a monkey out of me'. I just completely broke down. I had a fortnight's leave and they sent me to Leeds University and an amazing thing happened here. When I reported in, the first person that I bumped into was RSM Tommy Green of the Durham Light Infantry.

We stared at each other and he said, 'Mole, how the hell did you get here?' I said, 'Tommy, do you know the last time I saw you? You were outside the German Commandant's Office along with ten others, and among you was Major Brook-Moore. You were being repatriated. If you can remember a working party strung out nearly in single file – a French working party – I was the second one in that party. I escaped and got back home.' He said, 'Well, of all the miracles, Mole.'

142

From there I was sent to Arborfield and it was here on the square one day that the company was called to attention and it was given out by the RSM that Staff Sergeant Beeson would report to the Officer Commanding the 19th AA Workshops Company REME, the subject being investiture, that Staff Sergeant Beeson had been awarded the Military Medal for Gallantry in the Field. I went to the office and I think I met Captain Payne representing the Officer Commanding and this was 21st July, 1945, and he gave me a letter from the Under Secretary of State, The War Office, Whitehall, London, and it said that Staff Sergeant Beeson was to report to Central Chancery of the Order of Knighthood, St. James's Palace, SW1 at the hours of 9 to 9.45 hours on 23rd July, 1945. I went to the QM stores and was issued with a new battle dress uniform, new boots on which literally I spent nearly thirty-six hours non-stop brushing and boning to get a polish on them and my toe-caps were like patent leather. I took my wife, and my sister and we marched across the square at Buckingham Palace, and went through the big doors into a salon where there were two orchestras. My sister and my wife sat in the front row. There were several of us who were to be decorated for one award or another and I was taken to the library, and there I met the Earl of Clarendon. He gave us a lecture on how we were to present ourselves to the King – that we were to march to him, come to attention, do a sharp left turn, take one pace to the rear. There was another high ranking officer by the side of the King.

My name was called. I came to attention and he pinned the Military Medal on me. We were told by the Earl of Clarendon that when the King shook hands with us we were only to very gently shake hands.

I was very fortunate. His Majesty said to me, 'Staff Sergeant, where did you win your award.' The King spoke very slowly and his voice was weak. I answered him, 'With the French Resistance and escaping from occupied country, sir.' He then said, 'You have done a very wonderful piece of work. Thank you very much.' I then said, 'Thank you, Your

Majesty,' and then taking one pace to the rear, took a right turn and walked smartly off.

And that was the climax of my adventures. I had been through hell and I had had to use my brains and help from friends and I knew a lot more about the world than I had six years before.

THE END